Primary Education and Society

Stuart Marriott
University of Ulster

 The Falmer Press

(A member of the Taylor & Francis Group)
London and Philadelphia

UK   The Falmer Press, Falmer House, Barcombe, Lewes, East Sussex, BN8 5DL

USA   The Falmer Press, Taylor & Francis Inc., 242 Cherry Street, Philadelphia, PA 19106-1906

First published 1985

Library of Congress Cataloging in Publication Data

Marriott, Stuart.

Primary Education and Society.

Bibliography: P.
1. Education, Elementary—Great Britain.
2. Education, Elementary—Social Aspects—Great Britain.
I. Title.
LA633.M35   1985   372.941   85-10388
ISBN 1-85000-070-0

Typeset in 11/13 Garamond by
Imago Publishing Ltd, Thame, Oxon.

Printed in Great Britain by Taylor & Francis (Printers) Ltd, Basingstoke

Contents

Acknowledgements

I would like to thank John Eggleston, Lesley Marriott, Valerie Morgan, Michael O'Hara and Bill O'Neill, all of whom read earlier drafts of this book and made very helpful comments.

I am also grateful for assistance, in a variety of ways, from Kay Ballantine, Sara Delamont, Rosemary McCollum, Ruth McGuckian, Hilja McMahon and Tom Whiteside.

Finally, thanks to my colleagues, especially past and present members of the LT5 mafia; this book owes much to their influence.

1   Introduction

This book consists of descriptions and analyses of aspects of primary education; its purpose is to facilitate a more sophisticated understanding of the processes and practices involved, from which informed opinions can be derived.

For many people such a project may seem superfluous; after all, everybody knows about primary schools. Nearly all citizens, at least in western countries, have spent several years of their lives in classrooms and primary schools are consequently among the most obvious and familiar features of our society. Adults know about schools in the sense that they have memories from their own childhood of the sights, sounds and smells of classrooms and playgrounds and perhaps recollections of unusually gifted or inept teachers; they may also gain impressions of schools from brief visits with their children and possibly from media reports concerning (very often) particularly notorious schools. As Jackson (1968) has argued, then, the attendance of children at primary school is such a common feature of our society that the adults who watch them go hardly pause to consider what happens to them when they get there, because in a sense they already know. Most of the time, 'we simply note that our Johnny is on his way to school, and now, it is time for our second cup of coffee' (p. 3).

But this apparent obviousness of primary education is misleading. Most adults' first hand knowledge of the everyday and ongoing work of primary schools and classrooms is in fact very limited. And even if parents make efforts to find out through their children what is actually happening in the primary school classroom, such second-hand knowledge may not be totally illuminating, as is suggested by Mills' (1980) 'play':

Act I

Location: A primary school somewhere in England.
Actors: A teacher and thirty children, including John.
Action: A maths class is in progress.
Three masked raiders enter and demand the dinner money. Swift Kung-Fu-type blows from the deputy head render them helpless and they are carried off. Maths continues, with estimates first, then calculations, on the amount of money the thieves might have stolen. Lightning strikes the weather cock on the school roof. It crashes through the ceiling, scattering debris about the room. When the dust settles, the children sweep away the rubbish and then write about the experience in their daily diary.

During dinner time, a mad dog, foaming at the mouth, rushes around the dining room, savaging one of the infants' dolls.

The art lesson in the afternoon captures the incident in paint, clay and collage. Then, relaxation at the end of the day with the book, Fearsome Frankenstein Fables.

The bell sounds, Home time.

Act II

Actors: John and his mother at tea.
Action: Mother: What happened in school today, dear?
John: Oh, nothing. (p. 1)

Although most adults are familiar with primary schools only in rather limited ways, they tend to hold opinions about them, often very strong opinions. They may feel that present day schools compare unfavourably with those of the past in that, for example, teachers are not strict enough, or that children 'just play with bricks all day' (Sharp and Green, 1975, p. 202) or, seemingly more rarely, that children in schools today receive a fuller and more complete education than their own. Clearly, opinions are held strongly because in industrialized societies education *matters*: it is in the view of most citizens a crucial phase of life, one which is likely to have a great influence on occupation and career and thus directly and indirectly on the whole of adult life. Education is thus very important, and many parents expect primary education in particular to achieve a great deal for their children.

It is not only educational laymen who express strong views about primary education. Equally forceful and idiosyncratic opinions can often be found in the writings of professional educators. We may, for example, compare the ideas of Robinson, a late nineteenth-century school inspector, with those of the influential and prestigious Plowden committee some ninety years later:

> A good school prevents crime, and thereby adds to the value and security of property, and forms beneficially the manners and character of the people. A teacher has it in his power to plant sedition and discord, to sow treason and corruption, irreligion and immorality, and, frequently, to unite the people together for evil; or he may cultivate allegiance to the sovereign, obedience to God, and respect for our fellow-man. (Robinson, 1876, p. 316)

> The school sets out deliberately to devise the right environment for children, to allow them to be themselves and to develop in the way and at the pace appropriate for them. It tries to equalize opportunities and to compensate for handicaps. It lays special stress on individual discovery, on first hand experiences and on opportunities for creative work. It insists that knowledge does not fall into neatly separate compartments and that work and play are not opposite but complementary. A child brought up in such an atmosphere at all stages of his education has some hope of becoming a balanced and mature adult and of being able to live in, to contribute to, and to look critically at, the society of which he forms a part. (Central Advisory Council for Education, 1967, pp. 187–8)

Perhaps an initial reaction to these two quotations is that in the space of ninety years or so views of the purpose and nature of primary education have changed dramatically, especially in that Robinson's stress is mostly on the teacher whereas Plowden is in some sense child-centred in approach. While not wishing to minimize the real differences here, it is also interesting to note what is similar in the attitudes of the two writers. Both adopt a tone of confident assertion; both *know* what a good school is like. Both at least implicitly exhort schools to do better and both are extremely ambitious for schools: that they should attempt to achieve presumably extremely difficult goals, whether they be obedience to God or a critical attitude to society is assumed without question. Both assume that schools and teachers are powerful agencies, that they *can* either equalize opportunities or prevent crime, as the case may be. Both take a view of education as being more than just the dissemination of knowledge, however defined: schools are also legitimately concerned with values (or 'character'). And finally, neither, at least in these extracts, provides a scrap of evidence to substantiate their rather large claims — indeed it would be difficult to imagine what kinds of evidence could be mustered to demonstrate (or disprove) connections between schools and such vague entities as 'balance', 'discord', 'corruption' or 'maturity'. A great amount of the writing about education, including primary education, is of this kind: opinionated, assertive, exhortatory, ambitious; it has indeed been suggested that this is one reason why a succession of fads and fashions arise in education: 'Never run after a bus, a woman or an educational theory — another will be along soon', (quoted by King, 1978, p. 3), fashions which far outpace the provision of adequate evidence.

Thus, the general public, particularly interested groups such as parents and employers, as well as those professionally concerned with education but outside actual schools, hold strong but often conflicting views about the nature and purpose of primary education. All such groups increasingly have some means both of articulating their ideas (for example through current moves towards making teachers more accountable). From the point of view of the practising primary school teacher such developments may appear very challenging, or perhaps even threatening. One response to this situation is for the teacher to retreat behind the classroom door and immerse herself in the consuming and exhausting business of day-to-day work with children, on the principle that if one ignores a problem long enough it will eventually go away. Such a response is understandable but there is an obvious danger that vague and incoherent views about primary education may cause problems: confused, inaccurate or misleading ideas, if unchallenged, may yet form the basis of both individual and collective decision-making about educational practice. But if, on the other hand, the teacher becomes sufficiently well informed to be able to argue coherently for the educational principles and practices she is committed to, not only may this be professionally beneficial in itself, but it may contribute to a broader and deeper understanding of primary schools among members of the public interested in education, and perhaps especially among parents. This book is for the teacher, potential teacher or other interested person who favours the latter course of action, and wishes to learn more about the intricate processes of primary education.

Sociology and Primary Education

There are many ways of generating an informed understanding of primary education (it could be attempted by means of the procedures and concepts of psychology, economics, philosophy or politics, for example) but here we will utilize the perspectives of sociology to provide a unifying framework for our analysis. This is not the place for a detailed account of the discipline of sociology, or even of sociological approaches to education (Davies, 1976; Robinson, 1981; Meighan, 1981; and Woods, 1983 are four among many recent texts providing useful introductions), but central to sociological enterprises is the attempt to *understand* social phenomena, including schools and classrooms, and the attempt to *explain* why such phenomena have the characteristics they do have at this time in this society. However, at the present time there are some 27,000 primary schools in the UK containing several million children and hundreds of thousands of teachers, and it would be impossible to provide even the most superficial account of the uniqueness and individuality of all these people and schools. How, then, given the diversity and heterogeneity of people and institutions involved in primary educa tion, is it possible to construct an account of the social? Perhaps Midwinter's (1974) observation provides an initial clue:

> Having visited hundreds of primary schools ... there is a depressing uniformity despite the much vaunted autonomy allowed heads. The assembly, those early-morning maths, the milk break, the values, the rules, the art-work, the reading schemes, the hymns, the staffroom conversation, the requisition, the lavatories, the school dinners, the knot of mothers at the gate, the registers ... these and so many more are much of a muchness. The overall institutional climate is constant. (p. 70)

In spite of the enormous variety of schools teachers and children, then, it is possible, even inevitable, that there are areas of consistency and uniformity, common practices and routines, similar styles and methods (which from Midwinter's standpoint seem depressing) that transcend local and individual differences. In other words there are *patterns of action and interaction*, and a central aspect of the sociologist's task is the discovery and understanding and explanation of such patterns. From this it is clear that essential elements of a sociological approach are that it attempts to be both *empirical* (based on evidence) and *theoretical* (concerned with understanding and explanation). In addition, sociological approaches attempt to be *objective:* the extent to which this is possible or indeed desirable is perpetually a matter of fierce controversy in sociology, but for present purposes it is essential in the sense that the analyses in this book attempt to be distanced from, and more than, one individual's account of his perceptions of aspects of the social world (see Berger and Kellner, 1981, for a more developed discussion of this issue).

There would seem to be three reasons why such an approach to primary education may usefully play a part in the generation of informed understanding. Firstly, it can provide a sense of the context within which teachers and pupils work. Teachers can become so immersed in the minutia of classroom life that events and processes that influence them and their work but which occur outside the classroom door are neglected. It may, however, be very useful for teachers to understand the structure and organization of primary education within which their classroom work takes place. Thus, we shall look at some of the factors which account for the existing structures of schooling, and those which currently affect and sustain primary education.

Secondly, primary education is dynamic not static, changing partly in response to social and economic changes in general, but also in response to changing ideas and beliefs (or ideologies) concerning the nature and purpose of schools. Although there is unlikely to be an exact correspondence between such opinions and beliefs and actual practice in schools, clearly the two are related. Examining changing ideologies is thus a means of assessing the intellectual, political and social milieux within which primary education is embedded and of understanding further the ways in which primary education came to be as it is and is currently changing. As suggested earlier, it is important for teachers to be aware of the debates surrounding such ideologies in order to be able to make a critically informed contribution.

Thirdly, and perhaps of most practical significance to teachers, such an approach may illuminate the processes of schooling themselves. It is often hard for individuals, especially teachers relatively isolated within classrooms, to assess the extent to which practices taken for granted in one school are typical (or unusual) in primary schools generally. Further, classrooms are immensely complicated places; teachers may engage in a thousand interpersonal exchanges every day (Jackson, 1968, p. 11) and it is often very difficult for participants or even observers to stand back and make sense of what is apparently quite inchoate. For these reasons it may be valuable to examine such concepts as that of teaching style and evidence about the different effects of particular styles. More broadly, it may be useful to look at such issues as what is taught in primary schools — and what is learnt; what experiences and perspectives teachers and pupils bring to the classroom, and what strategies they use to interact and negotiate with each other when they get there; how such strategies have changed and are currently changing; and what is the relationship (if any) between the minutia of classroom interaction and wider social processes.

Thus in summary, this account will attempt to:
(i)   explain the current structures and organization of primary education in the UK;
(ii) understand why primary schools exist in the form and operate in the way they do;
(iii) consider some aspects of the process of teaching and learning in primary classrooms;
(iv) analyze the actions and practices of teachers and pupils in schools and classrooms;
(v)   assess the effects of primary schooling.

For a variety of reasons there are rather few sociological accounts which come to grips with these kind of problems and issues. In many respects Blyth's (1965) comment twenty years ago remains true:

> most of the research, and most of the general writing, in the sociology of English education has been confined to secondary and further education, almost as though sociologists thought that life began at eleven-plus. (p. 13)

Since the publication of Blyth's compendious account of primary schooling the sociology of education has, to summarize very crudely, prolifically spawned approaches of great variety, subtlety and complexity but few of them have been tested or applied empirically in primary schools (some exceptions will be discussed later). On the other hand there is a vast array of empirical work and research findings relating to primary school teachers, pupils, curricula, etc., written from within theoretical standpoints other than sociology or indeed from no overt theoretical stance. There is not, however, a substantial body of work which could be described as comprising the sociology of primary education and in many respects there has been little direct sociological attention to the area. For reasons of necessity, then, this account will tend towards the eclectic, but also for reasons of conviction: primary education comprises complex issues, and no single or simple approach will suffice.

Plan of the Book

In chapter 2 we will attempt to understand how the current structure of primary education and the current organization of primary schools evolved, by examining both the socio-economic forces and the ideological influences which have shaped the system. Chapter 3 is devoted to an examination of the Plowden Report and the debates which followed its publication. In chapters 4 and 5 we move inside the primary school and classroom to look in some detail at the practices of teachers and pupils. Finally, chapter 6 consists of an examination of competing accounts of the effects or primary education.

2 The Structure and Development of Primary Education

Definitions are difficult, but probably few would dissent from the view that primary education in Britain at the present time includes what happens to children aged between 5 and 11 under the supervision of qualified teachers in institutions called schools. While education does not only or even mainly occur in formal classrooms, for the present it is the conjunction of teachers and young children in schools which are the focus of analysis.

The Structure of Primary Education

Before looking at the development of primary education, a brief account of the current position may set the scene. The most obvious characteristic of the structural arrangement of primary education, as King (1983) has noted, is its diversity. Until recently there were three basic types of primary school, called infant schools (catering for 5 to 7 year old children), junior schools (for 7 to 11 year olds), and combined infant and junior schools, often called primary schools (for the whole 5 to 11 age-range). The introduction of comprehensive forms of secondary education, however, has among other effects altered the structure of primary education by giving rise to additional forms of pre-secondary institution, usually called first schools (age-range 5 to 8, 9 or 10) and middle schools (age varying in the range 8 to 14). There are also a few combined first and middle schools. Recent figures suggest that in England 49 per cent of primary schools are of the combined infant and junior type, 18 per cent are separate infant and 17 per cent separate junior schools, 15 per cent are first schools and 2 per cent are combined first and middle schools (Department of Education and Science, 1984a).

Most primary schools are publicly funded, or 'maintained', in some way, although what are called 'county' schools in England are financed differently from 'voluntary' schools which are usually of religious foundation, mainly Church of England or Roman Catholic. Some children (about 4 per cent of the total), however, attend independent primary schools or preparatory departments of secondary schools which are not directly funded by the state.

Another obvious characteristic of schools is the age and physical state of the building. Many schools are of nineteenth-century construction, others are newly built, with most somewhere in between. In all, around half of UK primary schools are of pre-1950 vintage and half were built after that date although there are regional variations. Styles of school building have also changed in the last twenty years from, in general, designs based on corridors and discrete classrooms to versions of so-called open-plan construction which, although varied, commonly dispense with at least some internal walls thus creating teaching areas rather than closed rooms (Cooper, 1981). It is likely that such open-plan designs now comprise between six (Bassey, 1978, p. 98) and 10 per cent (Bennett, 1980, p. 45) of the stock of school buildings and perhaps a further 30 per cent or more are what Bassey describes as 'semi-open-plan'. The physical condition of schools is difficult to assess objectively, but some indication may be gleaned from the English HMIs' observation that four out of five of the classes surveyed were in accommodation considered 'reasonably adequate' (DES, 1978, p. 9).

Schools' rolls, i.e. the number of children enrolled in a school, vary from less than twenty-five to over 800 but about four out of five schools are within the range of fifty to 400 pupils. The types of locality from which pupils come are difficult to define precisely but the HMIs estimate that about 17 per cent of the schools in their survey were in inner cities, about 45 per cent in 'other urban' areas, and some 39 per cent in rural localities. Certainly, and obviously, primary school pupils come from an enormous range of backgrounds, from homes situated in run-down inner city areas, middle class suburbs, new towns, housing estates, small villages, and communities on remote islands and hillsides. Obviously too, the children themselves are diverse in the extreme: for example, there are many children for whom English is a second language and many schools have substantial numbers of children from various ethnic minority groups (DES, 1978, p. 17). Because of vagaries of structure the age of children in schools is not always confined to the usual 5 to 11. There are about 400,000 children under the age of 5 in primary schools, sometimes in special nursery classes, and several hundred aged 12 or over, mostly in combined first and middle schools (DES, 1984a).

Not only are schools and pupils various, so are their teachers. About 180,000 full-time (and 16,000 part-time) teachers work in public sector primary schools in England and Wales of whom 139,000 or 77 per cent of the full-timers and almost all of the part-timers are women (DES, 1983b, p. 6 and 31). Women are particularly heavily represented vis a vis men in classrooms of younger children. Few men work in first schools in England (DES, 1982a, p. 63) and only some 400 teach in separate infants' schools out of a total teaching force in the latter schools of over 33,000 (DES, 1983b, p. 29); the HMIs report that 97 per cent of 7 year olds, 70 per cent of 9 year olds but only 51 per cent of 11 year olds in their sample were taught by women (DES, 1978, p. 15). Women are also over-represented on the basic salary scale (scale one) where there are eleven women to every man. Conversely, on the higher scales (two and three) and among deputy heads and headteachers men are increasingly common, to the extent that more men than women are heads of primary schools (a ratio of about 13:10). An increasingly large minority (currently some 18 per cent) of primary school teachers are graduates but most of the teaching force are 'qualified' teachers, i.e. they have attended a college of education or its equivalent and have emerged with a professional teaching qualification. Teachers also vary, obviously, in age and normally may be of any age between 21 and 65. However, there are currently relatively few teachers aged under 25 (7000), between 55 and 60 (13,000) and over 60 (5000); other than these exceptions five year age groups contain between 24 and 28,000 teachers (DES, 1983b, p. 23).

The Development of Primary Education in the UK

This pattern of compulsory primary schooling largely provided and financed by the state, in purpose-built institutions staffed mainly by female but entirely by qualified teachers has developed slowly and in some respects rather haphazardly over the last century. While there is a danger of oversimplifying complex issues, the history of the schooling of young children during the last 100 years can perhaps usefully be seen in the context of the theme of changing ideologies in a changing society. There has, in other words, been a fairly close relationship between beliefs about primary education and the economic and social structure of the society within which those beliefs have been held.

The concept of ideology itself is both complex and ambiguous; it is sometimes used to refer to sets of beliefs regarded as undesirable or misleading or false, in contrast to beliefs which are regarded as true which on such an interpretation are not ideological. For present purposes, however, the term ideology will be used to refer to any system of beliefs and ideas which legitimates the interests of organized groups; in this account we are briefly concerned to understand competing ideologies, not to attempt to demonstrate their truth or falsity. Many ideologies of, and in, education have been suggested, such as the three (progressivism, reconstructionism and classical humanism) described by Skilbeck (1976) but for the sake of simplicity it may be useful to confine discussion to two very broad networks of ideas about the nature and purpose of education. Various different labels have been suggested but here Evetts' (1973) terms 'progressive' and 'idealist' will be used to distinguish such themes in the development of primary education.

To summarize complex themes rather crudely, the idealist's stress is on such notions as the inculcation of high attainment in skills and subject knowledge via formal instruction and examinations. The idealist values the transmission of 'culture', is concerned about the maintenance of standards, and views the child as unsocialized, in need of discipline, training, and character building. In contrast, the progressive's worldview encompasses such ideas as the growth and development of the potentialities of the individual through child rather than subject centred teaching, pupils' learning from experience and by discovery, and essentially stresses drawing out from the child rather than imposing upon him.

However, educational concepts of these kinds do not exist in a vacuum; such ideologies of education are related to current and dominant political, religious, and economic ideologies and to the structure and organization of the society which they legitimate. While these relationships between education and society are not determined, one-to-one correspondences but rather form a loose and often very indeterminate fit, there is a broad consistency between ideas about and practices within schools on the one hand and aspects of the social and economic organization of society on the other.

Primary Education in the Nineteenth Century

Socio-economic changes in nineteenth-century society were particularly important factors in the increasing involvement of the state in the provision of schooling for young children. A major consequence of the Industrial Revolution was a perceived need for a disciplined and docile labour force for the rising factory system and, increasingly, a requirement for literate and numerate clerks and artisans. As the economy became more complex, differentiated and systematized, therefore, intellectual skills partly replaced physical strength as desirable attributes amongst the workforce. But schooling also had the purpose of inculcating appropriate habits and attitudes such as sobriety, diligence and regularity which were seen as essential for factory and office work. While such qualities were desirable for economic reasons they also had a further important role in that they contributed to the maintenance of the deep-rooted class divisions of Victorian society, and averted the revolutionary possibilities inherent in an increasingly educated and politically aware work-force. For such reasons, then, elementary education was based on the criteria of economic utility and of the maintenance of the existing social order; the 'payment by results' system introduced by Robert Lowe in 1862 was intended to ensure that teachers would teach and pupils would learn that, and only that, which fitted those criteria and at as little cost as possible. The pedagogical objectives of elementary education were summarized in evidence presented to the Newcastle Commission of 1861:

> (the pupil) shall be able to spell correctly the words that he will ordinarily have to use; he shall read a common narrative — the paragraph in the newspaper that he cares to read — with sufficient ease to be a pleasure to himself and to convey information to listeners; if gone to live at a distance from home, he shall write his mother a letter that shall be both legible and intelligible; he knows enough of ciphering to make out, or test the correctness of, a common shop bill; if he hears talk of foreign countries he has some notions as to the part of the habitable globe in which they lie; and underlying all, and not without its influence, I trust, upon his life and conversation, he has acquaintance enough with the Holy Scriptures to follow the allusions and the arguments of a plain Saxon sermon, and a sufficient recollection of the truths taught him in his catechism, to know what are the duties required of him towards his Maker and his fellow-man. (Maclure, 1968, p. 75)

A significant aspect of the philosophy underpinning such curricula was suggested by Joseph Lancaster, co-founder of the monitorial system, by which pupil teachers instructed younger children:

On the subject of order, and the necessity of it in all human affairs, the teacher may observe, *that order is heaven's first law*; and show the youth under his care, that the subversion of order, in the least degree, would produce confusion. (Johnson, 1976, p. 47)

Such economic and ideological constraints ensured that Victorian elementary schools were characterized by huge classes of children in dismal accommodation with few facilities, and rigid curricula accompanied by a harsh and authoritarian discipline. Williamson (1981) has provided an interesting account of the realities of elementary education in two mining villages. He suggests that in such schools teachers were poorly trained and resources were few. The grant based on performance by which schools were financed ensured a great emphasis on the transmission of the three Rs and encouraged teaching methods centred on pupils' rote learning:

The children of Heddon were treated to regular examinations. In the case of the upper standards, examinations were run on a fortnightly basis . . . and the reason for all this was a clear economic one. Inadequate performance in basic subjects could lead to the withdrawal of the grant. The inspector's report for May 26th, 1890, underlines the precariousness and urgency of the situation for the school; 'The Merit Grant is recommended solely on account of the epidemic, since elementary subjects were not up to the mark. Much better results of instruction will be expected next year'. (1981, p. 55)

Primary Education in the Twentieth Century

Slowly at first but with increasing speed especially since 1945, the elementary tradition has declined, to the point that in its original forms at least it has all but disappeared. Clearly, the social structure of post-war Britain is so different to that of the 1880s that parallel educational change was inevitable. The decline of rigidly hierarchical religious and social ideologies, the replacement of laisser-faire by collectivist economic philosophies, the achievement of universal suffrage and the rise of working class movements especially trades unions and the Labour party, urbanization and demographic changes, among many other factors, played a part. Perhaps particularly significant, however, was the demand for a much more highly skilled and adaptable labour force to cope with a complex and rapidly changing technological, scientific and industrial economy. Further, and increasingly, economic roles were allocated according to individual achievement particularly through education, rather than ascription (based on tradition or family background).

The history of primary education clearly reflects these changes. In the early years of this century increasing dissatisfaction with the limitations of elementary education, liberal educational ideas originating with thinkers and practitioners such as Montessori, Froebel, Rachel and Margaret McMillan, Dewey and Piaget, and the evidence of work carried out in nursery and infant schools and departments which had long been separated from classes of 'seniors' in the elementary school (originally so that the latter would not be disturbed in their work by the 'babies' [Whitbread, 1972]), coalesced into more progressive ideologies in education. These found their first official expression in the Hadow Report of 1931, called *The Primary School*, which in a famous paragraph declared that:

> the curriculum is to be thought of in terms of activity and experience rather than of knowledge to be acquired and facts to be stored. Its aim should be to develop in a child the fundamental human powers and to awaken him to the fundamental interests of civilized life so far as these powers and interests lie within the compass of childhood. (Consultative Committee, 1931, p. 75)

As Selleck (1972) argues, such progressive ideologies gained respectability in the 1930s, to the extent that informed educational opinion among staff in teacher training colleges, educational writers and theorists, and influential laymen like Hadow and R.H. Tawney, reflected such views. By 1939, then, progressivism had become the 'intellectual orthodoxy' but the impact of such ideas upon practice in schools was limited, even when the reorganization from elementary (all-age) schools to a primary/secondary system accelerated after the war. The new tripartite system of secondary education which emerged from the 1944 Education Act, largely based on psychological theories of the fixed and inherent nature of intelligence, with selection of pupils for different types of school, led to primary schools often being obsessively concerned with obtaining good results in the 11+ examination. Since the 11+ usually consisted of 'objective' tests of intelligence and tests of the three Rs, the curriculum of the primary school and the approaches utilized by teachers were constrained and limited in the interests of intense competition for grammar school places. In addition, the legacy of large classes, rigid streaming, and inadequate buildings and facilities which persisted into the 1950s and early 1960s, made new approaches difficult.

In a sense, then, the time was not yet ripe for the implementation of Hadow's ideas except to some extent in infants' schools and departments which, insulated from the competitive pressures of the junior school, were able to develop progressive practices, particularly in a few pioneering local authorities. In the 1960s, however, the education system as a whole became the focus of much greater public and political interest, partly because of the belief that education had clear and marked and desirable social, and especially economic, consequences; as Floud and Halsey (1961) suggested in their introduction to a collection of articles whose title of *Education, Economy, and Society* was itself indicative of this belief: 'Education is a crucial type of investment for the exploitation of modern technology' (p. 1). One consequence of such ideas was increased expenditure on education: for example, by 1969 6 per cent of the gross national product went to education, around double the figure of the mid-fifties (Kogan, 1978, p. 16). While some of this increase is accounted for by demographic changes (more pupils in schools) and while the extra money was disproportionately allocated to older pupils, primary education also benefited. For example, the current UK average of pupils to teachers is around twenty-three, although generally class sizes are higher than this since often some teachers (for example, the head) are not class teachers: in England some 60 per cent of all pupils are in classes of between twenty-six and thirty-five children; fewer than 5 per cent are in classes of thirty-six or more (DES, 1984a). In contrast, Douglas (1964) estimated on the basis of his survey that in 1957 45 per cent of primary school children were in classes of forty or more.

But not only did increased funding of education have an impact: broader social changes also had indirect but pervasive implications. The notion of the 'permissive society' is too vague to be of much value but it nevertheless does point to some real differences between the 1960s and preceding decades. Economic prosperity, liberal legislation, and perhaps a loosening of traditional social constraints leading to a diffuse sense of the importance of individual autonomy and a distrust of authoritarian approaches and solutions, resulted in a belief in the ability of a liberalized form of schooling to have a positive role in the achievement of further desired social change, economic progress, and individual fulfillment. Thus perceptions of and expectations from education changed; before the war opportunities for secondary and higher education were severely limited for ordinary working people but by the 1960s education became seen as the means by which a much larger proportion of the population could achieve both personal happiness and financial well-being.

Such factors resulted in changes in the structure of the education system, such as the abandonment of selection at the age of 11 (in most but not all areas of the UK), the introduction of comprehensive forms of secondary schooling, and the expansion of higher education. In addition, an educational climate emerged in which innovatory practices were seen as desirable or at least acceptable. The structure of primary education thus changed in response to changes elsewhere; and at the same time the possibilities of incorporating progressive practices in primary schools were given massive official encourage- ment by the publication of the Plowden Report (Central Advisory Council for Education, 1967). Because, in a sense, subsequent ideological debate in primary education has largely occurred in response to or denial of Plowden's ideas it requires more detailed examination; before doing so, however, this brief chronological account can be completed.

Primary Education since 1970

Since the early 1970s the social and ideological context of primary education has changed substantially. While it is difficult to disen- tangle all the significant factors, the terms 'contraction' and 'control' summarize many developments. Economic recession and financial stringency since the so-called Oil Crisis of 1973 have led to a situation in which the education system as a whole has had increasingly to compete for scarce resources. Unemployment has risen sharply (Plowden's comment that it 'has been almost non-existent since the war' (p. 29) seems now to be from another world), and inflation has become a crucial political issue. In such circumstances, pointed questions have been asked about the socio-economic pay-off from schooling and issues of cost effectiveness have begun to be raised much more insistently. At the same time demographic changes, with a decline in the number of pupils in schools, has meant a reduced demand for educational services and thus a significant slowing of the rapid expansion of the system in the 1960s. In 1964 in England and Wales there were 876,000 live births, which fell to 569,000 in 1977; similar falls occurred in other parts of the UK. Inevitably, a few years on from each date, primary school enrolments were affected by such demographic changes. In the early 1970s the number of primary school pupils in England was over four and three-quarter million, but by 1983 the figure had fallen to around three and a half million. Similarly, while in 1974 there were 188,000 (full-time and equivalent part-time) teachers in primary schools, by 1983 there were only 158,000 (DES, 1984a). Numbers of teachers and pupils have continued to decrease slightly since 1983, and according to recent DES figures little increase is likely until towards the end of the 1980s.

Such changes have had substantial and continuing effects: teacher training has been reduced, many small schools have been closed, teachers have begun to be redeployed or even made redundant, and the financial constraints on schools have become tighter. But perhaps even more important than these material factors have been more subtle changes. At a time of economic and educational expansion and optimism it could be argued plausibly that the two were causally related, that in fact investment in education had desirable economic consequences. But when the economy is no longer expanding or is even in decline, arguments for the direct economic benefits of schooling seem much less convincing. Similarly, uncertainty has grown about whether in fact education has tended to equalize economic opportunities or enhance social mobility (for example, Jencks *et al*, 1972). Indeed the ability of schools to achieve any of the profound social objectives envisaged by educational reformers and innovators has been questioned (cf Whiteside, 1978) and, to put the matter crudely, the notion that 'schools make no difference' has gained currency, at least among writers about education. From the point of view of pupils and students also, not only are educational qualifications no longer an almost automatic passport to secure and rewarding employment, but subjectively education's ability to contribute to personal fulfilment and happiness seems decreasingly certain; as Bernbaum puts it in a book provocatively titled *Schooling in Decline*, our 'romantic hopes that fragmented, industrialized and nullified man might at last come in from the cold' (1979, p. 15) may have been delusory.

Such factors have given a hard edge to recent educational debate and in particular have sustained what might be called a 'populist conservative' approach to schooling, typified by the series of several so-called 'Black Papers' (for example, Cox and Dyson, 1969a and b; Cox and Boyson, 1977). Partly in reaction, and partly for rather similar reasons of disillusionment with mainstream schooling, the 1970s saw the emergence and advocacy of a bewildering variety of radical alternative educational practices such as free schooling (for example, Head, 1974), deschooling (Illich, 1972), and no schooling (for example *Education Otherwise*, Meighan and Brown, 1980) and alternative theories such as those of the 'new' sociology of education (Young, 1971) and of a reasserted and reconceptualized marxism (for example in relation to primary education, Sharp and Green, 1975). Both of these latter approaches were highly critical of orthodox social democratic thinking and both tended also to be pessimistic about the outcomes of formal schooling.

In terms of policy, however, the contraction of the system plus doubts about the effectiveness of schooling have led, and increasingly appear to be leading, to attempts to wrest a greater degree of control over questions of curriculum, pedagogy and evaluation from individual teachers and headteachers and from bodies dominated by teachers. Education is more and more being held accountable through, as Richards suggests:

> politicians bringing the curriculum back into the public arena, through more interventionist policies by local authority corporate managers and elected members, through the rediscovery by some school governors of their powers and responsibilities under the 1944 Act and through parental pressures for greater information about schools and for participation on governing bodies. (1982, p. 20)

While all of these factors are significant, perhaps the most important is the clear determination of central government to take a greater degree of control over educational policies and practices. While such attempts have been evident in all phases of education, a number of innovations seem to have specific implications for the control and management of primary education. For example, the last few years have seen the establishment of the Assessment of Performance Unit, moves towards the notion of a core curriculum which all pupils would experience (DES, 1980 and 1981), the energetic promotion of certain subjects (for example, computer-based learning) within the primary school curriculum, but not others (for example, French), the greater extent of inspection of schools both singly and collectively and the publication of reports of such inspections, the abolition of the Schools Council, and greater governmental interest in and influence on the process of initial teacher training and the probationary year (DES, 1982b). Two of many recent government papers may be examined briefly as evidence of the government's intentions in some of these areas. The White Paper *Teaching Quality* (HMSO, 1983) provides details of plans to control more closely entry to and the management of the teaching profession. The paper proposes that courses of initial teacher training will only be approved if they fulfil certain criteria, such as that they should contain 'subject' content deemed appropriate to the primary school curriculum. Students should be selected for training on the basis of personal qualities as much as academic achievement, and practising teachers should be involved in the process of selection. Teachers will be more closely confined to work within the phase of education, and the school subjects, for which they were trained. Primary school teachers should specialize in some aspect of the curriculum to a greater extent than at present, and teaching performance in the classroom should be formally assessed by headteachers; teachers whose performance was unsatisfactory might be dismissed. Teachers will be more frequently redeployed, or even made redundant, in the interests of the efficient management of the teaching force as a whole.

These proposals may or may not be reasonable attempts to improve 'teaching quality', but that is not the point at issue: rather it is that until recently such matters have been regarded as largely the responsibilities of individual schools, institutions of teacher education and local authorities, and not ones with which central government should be closely concerned. Similarly, the HMI discussion documents *Curriculum Matters* are explicitly intended to contribute to the formation of a common framework of curricular aims and objectives. The first in the series is devoted to English (DES, 1984b), and lays out specific age-related objectives for attainment in the skills of reading and writing, listening and speaking, and in knowledge 'about language', together with principles for testing and assessment. The clear intention of the document, then, is to move beyond advice based on descriptions of good practice towards the production of a set of prescriptive, and national, guidelines. Once again, the aims and objectives in the paper may or may not be appropriate, but the publication of such detailed and specific recommendations by the DES represents a new development.

Thus a shift in the balance of control of schools away from teachers and headteachers in schools and towards greater centralization can be discerned. More broadly, it could be argued that such changes, with those in other phases of education, represent evidence of a fundamental movement from ideologies influenced by progressive ideas towards a set of neo-idealist educational assumptions, in which the demands of the market economy play a central and overt role. At present it is unclear to what extent this is a permanent or merely a temporary shift; the future is as always uncertain.

Conclusion: the Development of Primary Education

While this account of some aspects of the development of primary education and its associated ideologies in the UK has been of necessity very brief, it is possible to see a gradual movement from versions of an idealist towards versions of a progressive ideology of education at least among proponents of educational ideas and contributors towards educational debate and at least until the mid-1970s. Such a long-term shift reflected changes in society from one in which basic literacy and numeracy were sufficient skills for employment in adult life to one in which schools, including primary schools, were increasingly required to equip pupils with additional and much more complex accomplishments. Plowden represented the culmination of this process, embedded as it was in social and educational circumstances particularly favourable to advocacy of progressive ideas and practices. Since the early 1970s, however, increasing economic austerity and consequent ideological reassessment has led to scepticism about the efficacy of the school system and increasing insistence that it should justify and be seen to justify its practices in terms of economic pay-off.

Summary

This chapter has briefly examined the historical context within which state provided primary education has developed. Two themes run through the account: firstly that the nature of the schooling made available to young children has reflected the social and economic conditions of the time, and secondly that the history of primary education can be viewed in terms of a slow shift from idealist towards progressive ideologies of education. However, while the former theme remains germane, in respect of the latter a process of re-orientation may currently be taking place.

3 Plowden and the Plowden Debate

The Plowden Report

In order to examine more closely current practice and the ideologies which legitimate it in the UK, it may be useful to consider in some detail the debates surrounding the Plowden Report, since such controversies encapsulate differing views of the nature and purpose of primary education. As suggested earlier, the middle of the 1960s was a time in which the socio-economic and ideological context of primary education was particularly conducive to optimistic and expansionist thought. As Simon (1981) has observed, the Plowden Committee implicitly assumed:

> continuous economic growth, full employment, enhanced affluence and the more or less inevitable emergence of a more egalitarian society, where human potential, which they saw as unlimited, would find realization ... This was, perhaps, the last point in time (1965/66) when a general optimism expressed something of a consensus. (p. 15)

A liberal optimism, then, provided the context for the Committee's educational ideas which advocated and elaborated a progressive view of the nature of children, schools, and the structure of the education system.

Plowden was the last in a series of major post-war reports on sectors of education, following in particular Crowther on 15–18 year olds in 1959, Newsom on 13–16 year olds in 1963 and Robbins on higher education in 1963. As has been suggested previously, therefore, to some extent whatever Plowden recommended within its terms of reference ('To consider primary education in all its aspects and the transition to secondary education') would be pre-empted by earlier reports and consequent governmental action.

The Central Advisory Council for Education, under the chairmanship of Lady Plowden, deliberated from October 1963 and the Report was published in two volumes in 1967. It is a long and immensely detailed work which concludes with no less than 197 recommendations dealing with almost every conceivable aspect of the practice of primary schools. For present purposes, however, it is the beliefs, both explicit and implicit, which underlie the recommendations which are the focus of interest.

Central to Plowden's views are six assertions about children, schools and society:

(i) Our society is increasingly one in which understanding, critical thinking, adaptability and flexibility are valued, both for purposes of employment and for personal fulfilment.

(ii) Each child is a unique individual person developing and maturing physically, emotionally and intellectually at his own rate and in his own way.

(iii) Children are autonomously active and curious; the continuous interaction between the child and his environment from birth onwards implies that substantially the 'child is the agent in his own learning' (p. 194).

(iv) Because children develop individually they are at a stage appropriate for specific learning at different times; it is counterproductive to attempt to impose anything on a child until he is receptive to it. 'Until a child is ready to take a particular step forward, it is a waste of time to try to teach him to take it' (p. 25).

(v) Children's acquisition of such qualities and their cognitive learning arises most effectively from first-hand experience rather than having imposed on them abstract and impersonal knowledge: ' "Finding out" has proved to be better for children than "being told" ' (p. 460). Education is thus a process of enquiry and consequent self-realization, not an end-state.

(vi) Central to the purposes of education, therefore, is the *development of the potentialities of the individual child:* 'At the heart of the educational process lies the child' (p. 7) not only intellectually, but also in respect of the aesthetic, moral, social, and emotional.

Such ideas clearly had far-reaching implications for practice in schools and the Committee spelt these out in detail. Since all groups of children are composed of heterogeneous individuals developing and learning at different rates and in different ways, pedagogical techniques based on class teaching, and the practice of 'streaming, are inappropriate. Teaching and learning should be individualized as far as possible and based on the emerging interests of the child; school structures and organization should be flexible and open so as to allow and indeed encourage pupil-initiated discovery. Rigid traditional curriculum divisions are likely to be a hindrance to pupils' intellectual explorations and need to be 'cut across' (p. 197) or in part abandoned since children view their environment holistically. The teacher, who the Committee viewed as crucial, should 'adopt a consultative, guiding, stimulating role rather than a purely didactic one' (p. 198). In a school based on such principles competitiveness and external rewards (stars and marks and prizes), rigid timetabling, harsh discipline and corporal punishment, exercises and tests, would not be found.

While teaching and learning would ideally be completely individualized, clearly this is a state of affairs very difficult for a teacher to achieve in a class of thirty or more children; for this reason Plowden advocated the practice of grouping pupils for specific short-term purposes, groups which should be composed according to pupils' interest or attainment or needs but not be permanent (i.e. not intra-class streaming).

What then would a classroom influenced by Plowden's ideas be like? Galton *et al.* (1980) provide a summary sketch:

> The children are active, engaged in exploration or discovery, interacting both with the teacher and with each other. Each child operates as an individual, though groups are formed and re-formed related to those activities which are not normally subject differentiated. The teacher moves around the classroom, consulting, guiding, stimulating individual children or occasionally, for convenience, the groups of children which are brought together for some specific activity, or are 'at the same stage'. She knows each child individually, and how best to stimulate or intervene with each. In this activity she bears in mind the child's intellectual, social and physical levels of development and monitors these. On occasions the whole class is brought together, for instance for a story or music, or to spark off or finalize a class project; otherwise class teaching it seldom used, the pupil's work and the teacher's attention being individualized or 'grouped'. (p. 49)

This brief account of Plowden may be somewhat misleading; although the Committee undoubtedly were sympathetic to liberal and progressive educational ideas, they also kept their collective feet on the ground. Far from enthusiastically advocating a form of anarchic permissiveness, as some critics have alleged, the Report's tone is one of caution (it advocated 'neatness, accuracy, care, perseverance and the sheer knowledge which is an essential of being educated', for example) and its specific recommendations such as for the improvement of school buildings and the extension of nursery education are carefully thought out in terms of priorities, and the financial implications are considered. The Report did *not* prescribe or assume utopia, but rooted its proposals in what it saw as the best of current primary school practice.

However, Plowden did not only regard progressive approaches to teaching in primary schools and their structural and organizational concomitants as generally desirable but also strongly hinted that a large and increasing number of schools actually put them into practice: such schools represented a 'general and quickening trend' (p. 188). Further, the Committee asserted that the 'gloomy forebodings of the decline of knowledge which would follow progressive methods have been discredited' (p. 461). These two empirical assertions which were not adequately supported by research evidence and which have provided critics of Plowden with much ammunition, quite apart from the debate about the coherence of the Report's ideological position, will be examined later.

As suggested earlier, Plowden represented a legitimation of ideas that were not in themselves novel. Its major intellectual impact was probably to give confidence to teachers and others already attempting varieties of innovative and progressive practice. But the Report was not universally acclaimed, and criticism began almost immediately which in one form or another continues to the present time.

Critics of Plowden

R.S. Peters

An early response to Plowden edited by Peters (1969) was generally critical of the philosophical, psychological and sociological foundations of the Report although little is said in contradiction of its practical recommendations; indeed they are generally welcomed. Peters himself, however, is scathing about a number of the key ideas which Plowden utilizes, particularly those of children's development, the concept of self-direction which incorporates implicit stress on the value of personal autonomy and learning by discovery, the notion of the indivisibility of the curriculum, and prescriptions of self-effacing roles for the primary teacher.

In relation to the first, Peters argues that 'development' presupposes at least some kind of commitment to a view of what the end-product will be, some notion which can guide forms of development thought to be valuable. Most schools and teachers would rightly discourage some kind of development, regarding them as morally obnoxious; teachers hold beliefs about the relative *worthwhileness* of different activities and construct curricula on that basis: 'we do not offer blowing up live frogs with bicycle pumps or bingo as possible options' (p. 8). Thus education is most fruitfully conceptualized as the initiation of children into a selection of worthwhile pursuits, and the positive inculcation of valued forms of understanding. The concept of self-direction is inadequate for rather similar reasons; until they have at least a degree of experience of the skills and body of knowledge of a particular discipline, children cannot be capable of sensible autonomous learning: 'It is not enough, therefore, to say that children should learn to be themselves at school; we must give them the equipment to find out properly what sort of selves they want to be' (p. 12). Further, empirically, there is little evidence that 'discovery' is for all aspects of the curriculum an effective method of learning; intrinsic motivation is not necessarily sufficient. Regarding the curriculum, Peters argues that while traditional subject boundaries may hinder effective learning for some purposes, this is not true for all nor does it mean that such subject divisions are arbitrary. Rather, empirical research is required to establish whether or to what extent integration is of educational value; what is inadequate is the conclusion that because traditional subjects are often boring they should be abandoned in favour of topics or projects — the fault may be in the pedagogy not inherent in the subject. Finally, Peters criticizes the 'horticultural' view of the teacher as one who manipulates conditions so that the child can grow in his own way and at his own pace. Such prescriptions ignore the fact that children are social beings, that language and thought itself have social dimensions, and that children learn from other people; if the teacher stands back children will still do so, probably in less educationally desirable ways. Children learn effectively in a variety of ways and consequently no one pedagogical technique is appropriate for all circumstances; a justified reaction against authoritarianism should not lead teachers to refuse to intervene at all. Rather, teachers should be encouraged to develop a repertoire of methods of teaching, and should be encouraged to experiment in their use with different children.

S.H. Froome

The best known 'populist conservative' critique of progressive educational ideas is, as stated earlier, that of the Black Papers. However, the multiple authorship of these documents makes them somewhat incoherent, and they have already been much discussed by other writers, so it may be more informative to look at a systematic exposition of the case in relation to primary education written by one Black Paper contributor, S.H. Froome, in a book called *Why Tommy Isn't Learning* (1970).

In Froome's view, schools' curricula should concentrate on definable bodies of knowledge; central to education is the process of acquisition of facts: 'All knowledge consists of facts, and a step-by-step assimilation of these facts which are deemed desirable is the basis of learning' (p. 113). Such assimilation of facts is most efficiently achieved by children when they have mastered the basic skills of reading, writing and arithmetic, and it is these skills which have been adversely affected by proponents and practitioners of activity and discovery methods in primary schools. On the basis of his interpretation of some research studies, and much anecdotal evidence, Froome consequently asserts that children's attainments in such basic work have substantially declined since the war. Further, the attempt to replace the imposition by teachers of facts and skills on pupils by learning based on 'intrinsic motivation' is not only ineffective but is not likely to produce 'industrious, cheerful men and women' (p. 120) or good future citizens. The nature of children is such that they need teachers who demand high standards of work from their pupils, who have firm classroom control, and whose teaching style is one of direct instruction, to ensure that the dull and repetitive but crucial basic work of primary education is achieved.

Froome's response to Plowden is thus one of great scepticism. The Report's 'adulatory' recommendation of discovery learning is misguided because, without planning or structuring by the teacher, such spontaneous learning is likely in practice to degenerate into the spasmodic and haphazard pursuit of trivia; it is ridiculously inefficient and time-consuming for children to attempt the 'discovery' of well-known ideas and concepts, when the teacher can easily present well-organized and appropriate facts and information much more

quickly and economically — unless class sizes can be reduced to
around ten which would simply be too expensive.

P.S. Wilson

A very different response to Plowden is that of Wilson (1973). In his
view the concept of child-centred education involves freeing children
from as many constraints on what and how they learn as possible. He
contrasts this with Plowden's theoretical approach to children and
their 'nature' which is, he suggests, dominated by the perspectives
of academic child psychology. Three presuppositions are taken
for granted by Plowden: that children's nature can be adequately
described in terms of general and more or less inexorable laws; that
these laws are discovered by experts, notably child-psychologists;
and that education consists of fulfilling the psychological needs of
children which the experts have discovered. This, says Wilson, is
wrong: it assumes that children's mental development occurs in ways
similar to that of their physical growth; Plowden's whole approach is
physicalist and rather determinist, seeing children as merely the
product of genetic and environmental factors. But children are not
simply the focus of such forces, they are active: all human beings have
minds of their own and cannot sensibly be viewed as passively subject
to generalized laws in the manner of inert objects. Children's acts
have meaning which can only be understood in terms of intentions.
For these reasons, a truly child-centred education would focus on the
individual as a whole person and would have to take seriously the
child's ideas about himself and his education. Plowden never does
this: rather, in a sense, the Report is centred on child-psychologists
rather than on children.

The Implications of Plowden

While a number of such more or less critical analyses of Plowden
appeared it is probably fair to say that the response of the majority of
educational writers to the Report was far less critical, particularly in
the years immediately following its publication. A large number of
works adopting, developing and indeed celebrating the ideas of
Plowden were published such as those of Marsh (1970) and Blackie
(1967), then an HMI, whose *Inside the Primary School* sold huge
numbers of copies for a serious book, and a series of descriptive

booklets by various authors under the collective title of *British Primary Schools Today* (for example, Cook and Mack, 1971). In another influential book, and rather typically of this genre, Razzell (1968) describes a day he spent with a progressive teacher and comments: 'When I left the school late that afternoon, I knew that I should never be the same again. I was wild with excitement. This was my Damascus Road Experience' (p. 31). More recently, however, as suggested earlier, apologists for Plowden have been on the defensive, especially in the face of harsher economic circumstances, increasingly powerful conservative educational ideas, and governmental policies unsympathetic to progressive practices. Pluckrose (1979) for example, headteacher of an innovative London primary school, has argued that while Plowden was right in its basic approach, its more radical ideas being balanced by advocacy of (much less widely quoted) traditional values, it has been misinterpreted and misused by a minority of teachers whose ineffective and dangerous practice provided primary education with a public notoriety which was quite at variance with the slowly liberalizing work of the majority of schools.

As is implicit in Pluckrose's comments, somewhat separate from the debate about the intellectual coherence and appropriateness of Plowden's ideas has been a series of assertions about what is actually happening in primary schools. It was suggested on the one hand, with some pride, that primary schools in general had adopted or were increasingly involved in the process of adopting versions of progressive methods derived from the ideas of Plowden, and that such methods were at least as, and probably more, effective than those of traditional kinds. Opponents of such practices, while concurring in the notion of a 'progressive takeover', viewed this with alarm as representing a dangerous and quite unacceptable trend.

Plowden's Evidence

The Plowden Report itself was one significant source for the belief that there existed a 'trend towards individual and active learning' (p. 202) in primary schools. The actual evidence provided in support of such an assertion, however, is rather ambiguous or at least imprecise. On pages 101–2 of Volume 1 of the Report the Committee discuss a survey by HMI of almost all the 20,664 primary schools then open in England, in which schools were divided into nine types ranging from 'In most respects a school of outstanding quality' (Category 1) to 'A bad school where children suffer from laziness, indifference, gross incompetence and unkindness on the part of the staff' (Category 9). The writers of the Report consider that the 5,802 schools in Categories 1, 2 and 3, containing about a third of all primary school pupils 'are quite clearly good'. At the other extreme, 1,337 of the schools, with just over 5 per cent of the total pupil population on roll, are in Categories 8 or 9, described as bad or 'out of touch'. This still leaves the majority of schools and children somewhere in the middle, many of which Plowden suggests are schools that are 'capable of improvement and should be improved'. In fact, it is very difficult to say anything coherent about these schools on the basis of the information provided. Category 7, 'Curate's egg school, with good and bad features', Category 6, 'Run of the mill schools', and Category 4, 'Signs of life with seeds of growth', are rather obscurely labelled, and it is not at all clear from such descriptions what exactly is being assessed, or how. Thus it may have been rather optimistic of Plowden to conclude that the distribution of schools is skewed towards their understanding of 'good quality'. At most, only schools in Categories 1 and 2, 10 per cent of all schools, could be described as having achieved all or most of the Committee's recommendations, with perhaps Category 3, 23 per cent of schools, being well on the way, and another somewhat indeterminate proportion showing some promise. Even these rather vague conclusions, however, seem to be partly contradicted by evidence from the 1964 National Survey of 171 schools which is presented in Volume 2 of the Report. Here, HMIs assessed schools' overall quality and their acceptance of 'modern educational trends' such as their 'readiness to reconsider content of the curriculum' and their 'awareness of the unity of knowledge' (p. 278) on five point scales, as follows:

		Rating of all round quality (percentage of schools)	Rating of schools' acceptance of modern educational trends (percentage of schools)
(i)	Very good	1	3
(ii)	Good	21	18
(iii)	Average	61	47
(iv)	Below Average	16	29
(v)	Poor	1	3

Once again, it is difficult to know what to make of this: it is unclear what reliance can be placed on an overall assessment of an institution as complex as a school on a simple five point scale, particularly as HMIs were instructed to 'allow for a national distribution' of (i) 5 per cent; (ii) 20 per cent; (iii) 50 per cent; (iv) 20 per cent; and (v) 5 per cent, which seems on the face of it to anticipate the findings. In view of this, HMIs appear to have assessed schools as more often average in quality (61 per cent not 50 per cent) and below average in awareness of modern trends (29 per cent not 20 per cent) than one would have expected. But the means by which HMIs assessed schools in these ways and the validity of such presumably highly subjective judgments is very unclear.

Interpretations of Plowden

However, it was generally the positive note struck in the text, rather than the detailed evidence that was taken up by subsequent writers, who developed Plowden's ideas while asserting, or more frequently implying, that dramatic changes were occurring not just in a few schools but in large numbers, and that further changes in the directions advocated by Plowden were both desirable and likely. Thus, to take two of many possible examples, Blackie (1974), an HMI who acted as 'assessor' to the Plowden Committee, wrote a book devoted to the elaboration of strategies for introducing and extending progressive practices in primary schools and stated that: 'the trend of change, founded upon experience in the classroom and initiated teacher-by-teacher and school-by-school, *has been* in the direction with which this book is concerned and *it has continued* because the results have been convincing' (p. 18, emphasis added). Similarly, Bassett (1970) asserted that 'primary education is undergoing major change' (p. 3) and devoted a chapter to describing the 'considerable ferment' (p. 27) he perceived in primary school curricula, organization and teaching methods, and concluded that: 'such are some of the ways *being taken* to make the curriculum more relevant, and the methods and organization more in harmony' (p. 57, emphasis added).

The impression of 'revolutionary' changes thus created, however imprecisely, by commentators more or less closely involved in primary education was taken up in different ways by at least four different groups or audiences. Firstly, writers wishing to advocate innovation in, for example, secondary schools pointed to primary education as the site of successfully accomplished change, thus reinforcing the impression that such changes had actually taken place. Hoyle (1975), for example, argued that in primary schools:

> The basic approach is developmental in that the stress is upon nurturing the growth of individual children through shifting

the balance from formal class teaching to the creation of
informal learning situations with an emphasis on exploration
... the transformation has been an informal, relatively un-
planned and more or less a spontaneous movement ... The
secondary school can certainly take lessons from the primary
school in terms of its general educational approach ...
(p. 342–3)

Thus the idea that a progressive 'transformation' of primary education had already been more or less unproblematically accomplished
was incorporated within accounts of other sectors of education.

Secondly, a number of American writers, dissatisfied with the
practice of elementary education in the USA, visited progressive
primary schools in Britain, and wrote books and articles about their
experiences with the explicit intention of persuading American
educators of the viability of such practices. The Anglo-American
Primary Education Project series *British Primary Schools Today* has
already been mentioned, but in addition work such as that of
Featherstone (1971), Rogers (1970) and especially Silberman (1970)
were published. Silberman's book, which sold more than 340,000
copies by 1973, and is reputed to have made a great impact on
teachers in America, is written in a journalistic style and portrays
schools largely in terms of a series of examples or 'items' which extol
the virtues of progressive methods. For example:

ITEM: An infant school in an abjectly poor, crime-ridden
cockney slum in London. Until a new young head converted
it to the free day approach, the school had been notorious for
vandalism and disciplinary problems. Eleven months after the
new head had taken over, I did not see a single disruptive
child in a half-day of classroom observations. (p. 229)

ITEM: A classroom in an infant school in a pre-1900 building
located in a deteriorating London slum; the school's population is 56 per cent immigrant. A six year old is reading to the
visitor, fluently and flawlessly, while two others are on the
floor, measuring the length of the visitor's shoe, and then
writing their findings in a little notebook ... (p. 236)

ITEM: An American visitor asks the Education Officer of a
large English school district, a man known for his passionate
advocacy of informal education, whether he has any statistics
on student achievement that might permit comparisons between informal and formal methods of schooling. 'Here are

the statistics', he says, as he opens an enormous leather portfolio lying on his conference table. The portfolio contains samples of paintings, drawings, collages, embroideries, poems, stories, and essays from schools in his district. (p. 257)

Through countless such anecdotes Silberman creates the impression that progressive practices are the norm. He concludes:

The joyfulness is pervasive: in almost every classroom visited virtually every child appeared happy and engaged. One simply does not see bored or restless or unhappy youngsters, or youngsters with the glazed look so common in American schools. (p. 228)

Silberman subsequently edited a massive *Open Classroom Reader* (1973) which included selections from work by Sir Alec Clegg, the distinguished Chief Education Officer of the West Riding of Yorkshire, titled *Revolution in the British Primary Schools*. Straight from the horse's mouth, this time, comes once again the assertion of profound educational change.

Thirdly, the belief that informality was sweeping through primary classrooms was taken up by populist conservative writers with increasing insistence, arguing, in essence, that such educational changes could be causally linked not only to a decline in educational standards (especially in reading and writing) but also to social unrest, increasing truancy, vandalism, violence and crime, the break up of the family, and what Boyson (1975) has called 'the decline in general culture'. For example, Froome (1970) argued that progressive and 'child-centred' methods have caused a decline in standards of discipline in primary schools, with dire educational and social effects. Pointing to statistics showing an increase in juvenile delinquency, he argued that this was largely caused by a relaxation of authority both at home and in the classroom. Classroom discipline has significant implications for adult citizenship: only by great stress on discipline in schools can the production of responsible and mature adults be ensured. Kemball-Cook (1972) in an article critical of Plowden, argued that a relaxed approach to discipline is particularly unsuitable for boys; while girls in primary schools exhibit docility and eagerness to please, boys' toughness and aggression requires firmer handling. Similarly, the apparently ubiquitous abdication of teachers in primary schools was connected by such writers to impending or current economic difficulties; for example, Cox and Boyson (1975) argued that if the non-competitive ethos of progressive education was allowed to dominate our schools, the result would be a generation who would be unable to maintain current standards of living when opposed by overseas competitors.

The fourth 'group' who began to take up the issues involved in this debate was sections of the mass media, especially the popular press, whose reports concerning education began to be unusually frequent and detailed. In normal circumstances education is a minority interest, the discussion of which is generally confined to journals like *The Times Education Supplement* or the reports of specialist correspondents in the so-called 'quality' press. In the 1970s, however, partly because of the controversy and newsworthiness created by the Black Papers, education became a much more visible topic of concern to the media. The treatment of education by the press between 1975 and 1977 has been interestingly analyzed by the Centre for Contemporary Cultural Studies (1981) who concentrate on the reports in two papers, the *Daily Mail* and the *Daily Mirror*, They argue that such papers adopted the rhetoric and the agenda of the Black Papers wholesale, viewing education as a metaphor for a more general social crisis. There was, they suggest:

> a shared structure of assumptions and definitions informing the contributions of the two papers to the newly prominent controversies around schooling. What was presented as a 'debate' was in effect a monologue concentrating on items concerning teachers' lack of professional competence or the negative aspects of pupil behavior ... 60 per cent of the 595 items in the sample concentrated on unfavourable accounts of school developments ... Images of incompetence, slovenly, subversive or just trendy teachers who had failed to teach or control the undisciplined pupils in their charge became too familiar to need elaboration. Background actors — wild-eyed theorists, out-of-touch bureaucrats and the complacent self-interested leaders of some unions — were as often sketched...
> These pictures crystallized the matter into a specific cluster of issues and of suggested solutions. The reforms of the 1960s, especially the introduction of progressive methods and of comprehensive, were held responsible for an alleged decline in general standards and basic skills, for a lack of social discipline and the incongruence between the worlds of school and work. (pp. 210–12)

The CCCS go on to suggest that the sheer weight of repetition of these accusations formed a process of circular validation whereby almost any event could be used to fit into the framework of assumptions, and counter-evidence, if not simply ignored, could be treated as a whitewash. Further, these themes were presented in tones and styles of confident conviction that such disquiets represented the views of the vast majority of ordinary citizens, especially parents: in such ways the media having generated a 'moral panic' were able to point to public opinion as reasons and support for calls to remedial action. While this is not the place for a detailed analysis of the role of the media in this area, clearly the fact that the press amplified and publicized the idea that dangerously progressive ('trendy') practices were sweeping through primary schools was important as one powerful example of more wide-ranging accusations about the state of education.

Thus, as suggested earlier, both proponents and opponents of progressive innovations concurred in the view that revolutionary changes were in fact occurring in schools. Advocates painted a picture of classrooms of self-motivated pupils working hard, choosing rationally, setting standards for themselves, cooperating together, learning through creative activities and discovery methods, and achieving high levels of intellectual performance, all apparently without coercion or even control by teachers. If this was a caricature of Plowden's ideas, it was, nevertheless, seized on by a variety of critics, who connected all manner of social discontents to the introduction of such ideas and practices into primary schools.

William Tyndale

At the same time, one particular primary school came to be seen as a classic example of all that the Black Papers and the popular press were campaigning against: William Tyndale Junior School, in Islington, a school which very publicly fell to pieces during 1975 and 1976. The case of Tyndale has been analyzed in detail in several books (for example, Gretton and Jackson, 1976; Ellis *et al.*, 1976) and articles (for example, Dale, 1979 and 1981) and by the report of an official enquiry (Auld, 1976), and the byzantine complexities of the case are not of present concern. Suffice it to say that many of the teachers, led by the Head, Terry Ellis, and the Deputy, Brian Haddow, whose educational views were undoubtedly radical, attempted to introduce changes in the school in the direction of what they saw as greater democracy and genuine choice for the pupils many of whom, they argued, unlike middle class children, were actively disadvantaged by schooling. Thus, as the teachers themselves put it, the philosophy underlying their actions was:

> democratic, egalitarian and non-sexist; it was concerned with children's social development, with their individual needs and achievements; it was geared to activity, not passivity; made no false distinctions between 'work' and 'play'; rejected arbitary (sic) standards of attainment and behaviour; asserted the necessity for a wide range of choices, the involvement of children in their own community, and exercise of positive discrimination towards the disadvantaged; and encouraged children to think for themselves, and gain the confidence to dominate material presented to them. Children were encouraged to ask questions, not conditioned to obey orders ... (Ellis *et al.*, 1976, p. 45)

In practice, some parents and most of the managers were uneasy about the changes which were made and children began to be withdrawn from the school. The managers attempted to intervene, and when rebuffed used their contacts in the media to gain widespread publicity for this 'school of shame'. The Inner London Education Authority (ILEA) decided to inspect the school; in response some of the teachers went on strike and set up an alternative school. Eventually a full-scale quasi-judicial enquiry was held which distributed blame widely among the teachers, managers, inspectors, and some ILEA officials. Five teachers were later dismissed and many of the other individuals involved resigned.

In many respects Tyndale was a catalyst of concerns connected with the control and management of schools, and its implications have reverberated through education ever since. But, more immediately, it provided a critical context for renewed assaults on the philosophy and practice of progressive schooling.

As the collapse of the school progressed, with its stories such as that teachers were using *Monopoly* to show children how to undermine capitalism (Gretton and Jackson, 1976, p. 22) the case of Tyndale was used as living proof that what had been said about progressive primary education was no mirage: it really was, it seemed, a case of crazed left-wing teachers indoctrinating young children with their pernicious, anarchic and destructive creeds.

Conclusion

There are several points worth considering about these debates arising, directly or indirectly, from the Plowden Report. First, the account provided here has probably exaggerated the rationality and coherence of the discussion: the nature of ideological exchanges, at least in education, seems to be such that most typical is invective and polemic, argument based on anecdote and gut feelings, and very selective approaches to evidence. The various Black Papers are particularly fruitful sources of such rhetorical outbursts (although they are by no means the only offenders) which often seem quite uncontaminated by contact with real schools, teachers and pupils. For example, it is difficult to see the assertion that progressive educational practice is epitomized by a classroom in which 'chaos reigns, all children doing exactly what they like' (Pinn, 1969, p. 101) as a serious contribution to an intellectually rigorous debate; rather, words like 'progressive', 'elitist' and 'egalitarian' have rapidly become multi-purpose terms of abuse.

Secondly, empirical evidence is relevant to many educational issues such as questions about trends of pupil attainment in particular skills, the effects of streaming, and so on, although even such questions are not at all straightforward. But in the heat of the debate research evidence has been used highly selectively in order to lend apparently objective support to an actually subjective account. The careful and thoughtful interpretation of relevant research in order to clarify the facts of the case before philosophical or political debate commences has been conspicuous by its absence (although a notable beginning has recently been made in the work of Richards (1980 and 1982), Blenkin and Kelly (1980 and 1982), and Alexander (1984)).

Thirdly, while it is tempting to regard the discussions of Plowden as in some sense representing differences and changes in opinion amongst, for example, teachers and parents in general, to assume so is probably a mistake. The debate has been carried out at a level and in ways not necessarily accessible to such groups, whose responses to changes in the structure, organization and curriculum of schools may vary radically from those of participants in such ideological exchanges. Teachers' and pupils' perspectives on schooling may not therefore coincide with the assertions and arguments outlined above; the importance of the latter positions lies largely in their impact on policy making at both national and local levels rather than as necessarily directly reflecting popular or professional opinion in general.

Fourthly, and crucially, discussions of the implications of Plowden have been confused by the fact that both critics and protagonists of the Report, whatever their disagreements, have generally concurred in the belief that dramatic changes had been and were taking place in primary schools in the direction of more progressive practices. The whole acrimonious debate has been, in a sense, predicated on this consensus, yet as will be argued in detail in the next chapter the evidence for such a belief is at best tenuous. It could in fact be argued that the whole issue has been misconceived: not only has the debate not necessarily been representative of professional (i.e. teachers') ideas and opinions, but it has also not reflected the actual practices occurring within schools. It may thus be that there is a great disjunction between what educational writers have argued should occur and what teachers continue to do.

The debate arising from Plowden has been a very muddled one, then, partly because of its rhetorical and polemical tone, partly because of the absence of any reasonably clear demarcation between the empirical and the evaluative and the proper contribution of each to the discussion, and partly because of its lack of contact with the perspectives and practices of those who work in educational institutions.

Summary

In this chapter the focus of attention has been on the Plowden Report and the debates which have subsequently surrounded it. The Report was written and published at a time of social and economic expansion and optimism: it extended and developed earlier progressive educational thinking. It argued for a greater focus on the individual child and his needs, and suggested that education essentially consists of the development of the potential skills and qualities of the child. The Report proceeded to draw out the implications of such a view for classroom practice in great detail.

While a number of critics expressed reservations about the Report, generally its ideas and recommendations were welcomed, especially in the years immediately following its publication. However, Plowden also asserted that not only were progressive ideas educationally valid, but that they were actually being put into practice by an increasingly large number of schools. This assertion was assumed to be true by both protagonists and antagonists of the Report's ideas, and was significantly taken up by writers and critics opposed to progressive methods, especially in the wake of the collapse of William Tyndale school in the mid-1970s. Plowden's optimistic and liberal account of primary education appeared decreasingly appropriate to the harsher social and economic conditions of the late 1970s and early 1980s.

In the next chapter some empirical evidence will be examined which is relevant to the question of the validity of beliefs in widespread progressive practice in primary schools.

4　*Organization and Pedagogy in Primary Schools*

In order to assess the accuracy of assertions about teaching and organization in primary schools of the kinds outlined in the last chapter we can first look at studies of the prevalence of relatively recent organizational innovations in primary education such as non-streaming, vertical grouping, team teaching and the integrated day, all of which were at least implicitly recommended by Plowden. Further, we can examine evidence concerning teachers' classroom practices: is it in fact true that in contrast to the traditional (and stereotypical) authoritarian and didactic pedagogue, teachers now operate in ways more consonant with the ethos of Plowden? Finally, we can look at the vexed and complicated issue of the effectiveness of different styles of teaching.

Organizational Innovation

Streaming

One of the few fairly thoroughly researched areas of primary school organization is that of streaming, the arrangement of pupils in discrete and permanent classes on the basis of 'ability'. In 1962, according to Jackson (1964, p. 15–19) 96 per cent of the 660 primary schools with more than 300 pupils (i.e. probably big enough to stream) that he surveyed did so and half the children were streamed by the time they left their infants' school or department at the age of around seven. The most usual criteria for deciding on an appropriate stream in junior schools or departments were class teacher's recommendation (79 per cent of schools utilized this criterion) and infants' school report (67 per cent) and school constructed tests and 'experienced judgment' were also particularly popular. Writing at about the same time Daniels (1961) showed that of 173 primary school teachers that he studied not one was opposed to the practice of streaming, although teachers differed in opinions about how 'ability' should be assessed. Both Jackson and Daniels come out in favour of non-streaming, although at that time research as to the effects of streaming varied in its conclusions. In 1963, however, a large scale study was initiated by the National Foundation for Educational Research under the direction of J.C. Barker-Lunn (1970) in order to provide some definitive evidence. She studied some 5500 junior school children and their teachers in thirty-six streamed and thirty-six unstreamed schools, and concluded that there was little evidence that a school's policy on streaming affected children's academic performance, although it did have complex effects on the emotional and social development of children of average and below average ability. But perhaps the most interesting finding was that while 90 per cent of the teachers in streamed schools approved of the practice, so did 48 per cent of the staff in unstreamed schools, who often created a 'streamed atmosphere' in their classrooms by arranging children so that different ability groups were seated in different parts of the classroom (p. 272–3). Recent studies have confirmed this latter finding. For example, Bennett (1976, p. 58) found that 31 per cent of the teachers in his study favoured streaming, and 'unofficial' streaming practices persisted — about a third of the teachers used some form of permanent ability grouping within the classroom.

In recent years the number of schools organizing pupils in the traditional streamed pattern has declined rapidly. Bealing (1972), in a study of 189 teachers within two local education authorities, found no streaming at all among classes taught by teachers in one area, and less than one teacher in five in the other area was teaching a streamed class. By the time of the follow-up study in the same schools (Boydell, 1980), streaming had completely disappeared. In a census of primary schools in Lancashire and Cumbria (Bennett, 1976, p. 58) only 13 per cent of the two oldest age groups were in streamed classes, and HMIs in England (DES, 1978) found that only 10 per cent of the nine year olds in schools big enough to stream (and 4 per cent of the total number of nine year olds) were in fact in streamed classes. Similar patterns, although without figures, are reported by HMIs in Scotland: 'Pupils are rarely streamed by ability these days' (Scottish Education Department (SED) 1980, p. 43) and in Northern Ireland few schools are big enough to stream in any event (Department of Education Northern Ireland (DENI), 1981).

However, recent evidence suggests that while permanent and

fixed ability classes have all but disappeared, other forms of ability grouping have become more popular. In a questionnaire study of 732 junior schools and departments, Barker-Lunn (1982) found that 25 per cent of schools formed classes based in some way on pupils' ability, often on the basis of 'part-streaming', i.e. running permanent remedial classes including children from different age groups alongside classes which were otherwise of mixed ability. Another fairly popular organizational pattern especially in small and medium sized schools was to promote more able and/or hold back less able pupils, producing a wider age range but a narrower range of ability in each class. Further, and regardless of whether permanent classes were organized on the basis of ability or not, many schools organized part-time ability related groupings — children would sometimes be withdrawn from their class into remedial (for the less able) or enrichment (for the most able) groups, or children would be 'set' into ability groups across the year group for certain areas of the curriculum, notably mathematics. About a third of large schools but few smaller schools 'set' to some extent, and a third of all schools used enrichment groups. Remedial groups were almost universal in large schools, but rather less common in small and medium sized schools.

Barker-Lunn's study deals only with the organizational arrangement of classes and groups on a school basis. There is, however, also evidence that ability grouping *within* classes is popular. The HMIs (DES, 1978, p. 31) suggest that such ability grouping is particularly common for 'three Rs' work — for 7 year olds, for example, 75 per cent of teachers grouped by ability for mathematical work, and 63 per cent did so for reading, but only 4 per cent constructed ability groups for science and even less for PE and art. In Scotland, work in maths and language is also often differentiated according to ability (SED, 1980, p. 44) and in Northern Ireland Trew (1977) suggests on the basis of a study of twenty-eight classrooms in one area that mixed ability grouping is much less popular than similar ability grouping (p. 54).

In general, then, while traditional streaming has almost disappeared, and three-quarters of classes are now fully mixed ability, a substantial minority of children are in classes which are ability related in some way. The withdrawal of children into special groups and the practice of 'setting', both forms of temporary streaming, appear to be increasingly popular. Further, even within mixed ability *classes* mixed ability *teaching* is not common in aspects of the curriculum such as maths and reading, although more frequent in other aspects of the curriculum.

The Integrated Day

The term 'integrated day' is one often heard in discussions of primary education, and indeed teachers often take up positions for or against it. Yet, as several writers have noted (Dearden, 1976; Boydell, 1978) the term is not at all clear. Take for example two definitions:

> a form of organization in which the *child* exercises a greater degree of choice about what he is going to do and when he is going to do it (Taylor, 1971, p. 51)

> the freeing of the school from an organized timetable (Allen, *et al.*, 1975, p. 7)

Clearly these two definitions may be compatible, but are not necessarily so — it would be possible to imagine a school without an organized timetable yet in which pupils' work remained highly teacher directed. Moran (1971) in a study of 181 teachers who attended a conference on the integrated day found, rather as one might expect, that the term integrated day was used to refer to very different forms of school organization in which pupils were engaged in several activities within the classroom. While the notion of pupil choice was found to be central to most teachers' accounts, many excepted 'three Rs' work, and pupil choice never led to a completely unbroken day. There is evidence, further, that the incidence of both pupil choice and less overtly structured organizational practices are fairly rare. Bassey found that only 2 per cent of 498 teachers of juniors in Nottinghamshire reported that their programmes were so varied that they could not provide a timetable. In both junior and infant classes traditional features of the school day such as assembly, morning and afternoon playtime, etc., had retained their popularity. In infant classes (281 teachers) for example, all but seven had fixed times for playtime (Bassey, 1978, pp 21 and 62). Bealing (1972) concluded that although teachers tended to use non-traditional forms of classroom layout — seating in groups not rows, teacher's desk not at front centre — teachers, nevertheless, controlled their classes so tightly that it was doubtful whether there was much opportunity for children to organize their own activities. By the time of the follow-up study (Boydell, 1980) the classroom had become an even more static place, with a further tightening of teacher control. There were, for example, even fewer opportunities for children to engage in independent work individually or in small groups outside the classroom and less pupil choice of seating. It seems unlikely, then, that the integrated day, however defined, has actually become a major organizational strategy in schools. But what of other fairly recently emerging ideas like vertical or 'family' grouping and team teaching? The same group of studies again provide some evidence.

Vertical Grouping

By vertical grouping is meant the practice of deliberately combining children of different age groups into one class. Such combination has been very common, if involuntary, in small usually rural schools where there are insufficient children to fill age-specific classes. However, some large schools choose vertical grouping for reasons of policy decision or organizational convenience. In infants' classes the practice seems to be popular. Bassey's survey showed that only 15 per cent of the infants' teachers taught a homogeneous age group, and as many as 57 per cent were teaching all three infant age groups (1978, p. 59); twenty-four out of eighty first schools surveyed by HMI organized mixed age classes as a matter of policy (DES, 1982a, p. 63). It may be, however, that the practice is at present declining in popularity, especially in classes of older children. While HMI (DES, 1978) suggested that in 1975–77 around 15 per cent of children aged 9 were in vertically grouped classes, Barker-Lunn (1982) has reported that in 1980 only 4 per cent of the junior school classes she studied were vertically grouped.

Team Teaching

Although as Dewhurst and Tamburrini (1978) have pointed out, there are several kinds of organizational practice commonly labelled team teaching, central to the concept seems to be the idea that teachers work cooperatively with a large group of children across class boundaries. In spite of energetic espousal by a number of writers, the practice seems to be rare. Boydell reports few cases, and Bassey found only 3 per cent of his junior school teachers working in pairs and a further 3 per cent in teams of three of four, proportions repeated among infants' class teachers. In first schools only twelve of the eighty studied operated team teaching (DES, 1982a, p. 64) and Trew (1977) found only one example of such work in her sample in Ulster. Cooperative teaching does not even necessarily occur in open-plan schools: Bennett and Hyland (1979) have reviewed a number of studies of such schools, and conclude that the traditional 'one teacher one class' form of organization shows little sign of withering away, and Bennett *et al.* (1980) suggest on the basis of their national questionnaire survey that teachers more commonly work independently than cooperatively in open-plan schools.

These studies of organizational innovation, then, demonstrate that schools have changed. Nearly all public sector primary schools now cater for pupils of both sexes (although there are still a few which cater for boys or girls only). Certain practices, notably streaming of a rigid traditional kind have sharply declined in popularity, but have to some extent been replaced by other forms of ability grouping. Some fairly recent innovations such as vertical grouping in infants' classes have taken root, but others (team teaching, the integrated day) have not generally caught on.

Pedagogical Innovation

Teachers' Classroom Practices

In terms of the practice of teaching and learning in classrooms, too, the evidence suggests that change has been patchy and fragmentary. For example, Bennett carried out a census of all third and fourth year junior teachers in Lancashire and Cumbria. He showed that teacher control of movement and talk was generally high; teachers on average talked to the whole class for a fifth of the time. For three-quarters of the time children worked on tasks set by the teacher, and a subject centred curriculum predominated: on average, less than a fifth of each week was devoted to such 'integrated' work as environmental studies, projects or topics, or periods of pupil choice. Tests were frequent, eight out of ten teachers required pupils to know their multiplication tables, and though few teachers reported discipline problems over half smacked children for disruptive behavior. Only 9 per cent of the teachers' attitudes and practices corresponded to those advocated by Plowden, and Bennett (1976) concludes that: 'a high degree of permissiveness does not appear to be the norm in primary classrooms despite assertions to the contrary' (p. 43). Similarly, Nash (1973) found that formal written seatwork was the usual pattern of work in the classrooms he studied in Scotland, and Bassey (1978) reports that the majority of teachers of junior classes in his study rarely permitted pupil-organized work — 37 per cent never allowed this and a further 38 per cent permitted it for less than six hours a week (p. 27). While

Bassey provides no direct evidence, it seems highly unlikely that such pupil-directed work is often allowed in areas of the curriculum defined by teachers as central — such as, perhaps, mathematics and language. Boydell (1978), too, summarizing her own and others' work, concludes that the so-called primary revolution is a 'myth'; reports of Plowden-type teaching have been greatly exaggerated, and rather few children have ever actually experienced it (p. 55). All three of the recent reports by inspectors on the present state of primary education conclude that teachers generally tend to concentrate too heavily on traditional styles of work in the 'basic skills', and argue that the curriculum ought to be broadened rather than that excessive reliance on Plowden-type practices should be curbed. In England, for example, about three-quarters of the teachers mainly used a 'didactic' approach (predetermined and specifically teacher directed) while less than one in twenty mainly used an 'exploratory' style (greater stress on pupil choice and self direction) (DES, 1978, p. 26–7).

Perhaps some of the most convincing evidence in this area is provided by a recent and intensive observational study of what teachers and pupils actually do in classrooms (as distinct from what they say they do), carried out at the University of Leicester under the generic title of the 'ORACLE' project (Observation Research and Classroom Learning Evaluation). Five classroom observers sat through more than a 1000 hours in fifty classrooms of 8 to 10 year old children in nineteen junior and middle schools in three local authorities. They recorded in great detail the behavior of teachers and pupils on specially designed instruments called the *Pupil Record* and the *Teacher Record*. The first book (Galton *et al.*, 1980) of four published so far reporting the results of the research contains a mass of fascinating information about the practice of teaching and learning in primary classrooms, but four conclusions are particularly relevant for present purposes. Firstly, the authors present evidence that demonstrates that a high proportion (some two-thirds) of pupils' time in class in spent on work in the 'basics', i.e. skills relating to language and mathematics. Secondly, the notion that primary school classrooms are characterized by disorder and confusion was simply not true: classes were tightly controlled by teachers and on average pupils spent some three-quarters of lesson time engaged with the set task — and this is a very high work-rate. Thirdly, the forms of teaching observed were primarily didactic in style and interaction with pupils was generally factual and managerial. There was rather little exploratory, stimulatory, probing or thought-provoking talk; rather, statements and questions were usually designed to ensure that children knew what to do, how to do it, and that they got on with it. Fourthly, although pupils were commonly seated in groups they usually worked individually on set tasks and it was very rare for co-operative work to occur. Thus the writers conclude:

> the general pattern of the traditional curriculum quite certainly still prevails, and has not changed in any fundamental way, let alone vanished. Such claims appear to have been founded in mythology ... 'progressive' teaching, if by this is meant teaching having the characteristics defined by the Plowden Report, hardly exists in practice (Galton *et al.*, 1980, p. 155–6).

The Impact of Curriculum Projects

Some further relevent if indirect evidence is provided by studies of the impact of the many curriculum projects constructed and disseminated during the 1960s and 70s. Proponents of progressive ideas pointed to the existence of such projects as evidence of change, and for this reason evidence as to the extent of their adoption in schools may be germane to the question of the frequency of utilization of progressive methods in general. The rationale of many projects involved changes in methods of teaching and learning in a particular aspect of the curriculum, such as towards a greater degree of pupil-initiated work. For example, a key idea behind the 'Nuffield Mathematics' project was that children must be given opportunities to make their own discoveries and to think for themselves; understanding in mathematics is not achieved by rote-learning of techniques and drills. Sutherland's (1981) study of the impact of twenty-four such projects in Northern Ireland primary schools is thus of interest. Questionnaires were completed by 173 headteachers and 846 teachers from 185 schools in the province. Of the twenty-four projects, only three were

| | *Percentage of target teachers:* | | |
Project	Familiar	Currently using	Ever used
Breakthrough to Literacy	76	36	42
'Children of God'	92	86	88
'Nuffield Mathematics'	56	34	39

Source: Sutherland, A (1981) *Curriculum Projects in Primary Schools*, Belfast, Northern Ireland Council for Educational Research. Derived from Table 3.2.1., p. 22

familiar (i.e. they had some first hand knowledge) to a relatively large proportion of the 'target' teachers for whom the project was specifically intended (for example teachers of 5–7 year olds, teachers in Catholic schools, etc.), and even these three were by no means in universal use.

No other actual project on the list (which included the apparently well known 'En Avant', 'Man: A Course of Study', and 'Science 5–13') reached a familiarity rating of more than 21 per cent or a rating of more than 13 per cent for use at any time, although the book *Mathematics in Primary Schools* (Biggs, 1965), the first curriculum bulletin of the Schools Council and a precursor of Nuffield Mathematics, was rather more well known and used. Of the three relatively popular projects, 'Children of God' is clearly a special case unique to Northern Ireland, and the figures do not reveal the fact that it is little known or used in state schools and virtually ubiquitous (having been officially adopted by the Roman Catholic hierarchy) in church schools — indeed, 96 per cent of such schools were currently using the project. While 'Breakthrough' and 'Nuffield Mathematics', then, were the only curriculum projects used both voluntarily and fairly widely, the patterns of use described by Sutherland suggest that they were used mainly as supplements to other materials — indeed, only 10.8 per cent of teachers reporting on the implementation of 'Nuffield Mathematics' and 34.8 per cent on 'Breakthrough' used it as a main scheme. Sutherland concludes that such projects:

> were often having to compete with more traditional and structured schemes in reading and mathematics. In such cases only the elements that could easily fit in alongside the more traditional schemes were retained and sometimes only these elements had ever been adopted. (p. 148)

In England and Wales Streadman *et al.* (1978) suggest that projects in general were somewhat better known, and specifically 'Science 5–13', 'En Avant', 'Communication Skills in Early Childhood', and 'Nuffield Junior Science' were both more familiar and more commonly used than in Northern Ireland. Even here, however, according to headteachers, rather few schools used more than one or two of the range of projects available, and individual projects were not very widely familiar. For example, less than half of primary school teachers had even heard of 'Science 5–13' and only 17 per cent of teachers of 3 to 6 year olds had ever used the 'Communication Skills' project, in spite of the 'emphasis placed on dissemination by the Schools Council since 1972/3' (p. 37).

The evidence thus suggests at most a cautious and partial implementation of ideas and materials from innovative curriculum projects, often alongside more traditional approaches, and perhaps more frequently ignorance or non-adoption of such projects.

Teaching in 'Progressive' Schools

Also relevant is a study which suggests that in those rather uncommon schools where teachers have adopted progressive methods, openness, choice, discovery and so on are only part of the story. Berlak *et al.* (1975), puzzled by accounts such as that of Silberman of classrooms free of conflict and coercion, observed interaction in three schools locally regarded as progressive for several weeks each, and for shorter periods in thirteen other schools. They argue that three central 'dilemmas' of schooling exist: (i) teacher making learning decisions for children *versus* children making learning decisions; (ii) intrinsic *versus* extrinsic motivation: and (iii) teacher setting and maintaining standards for children's learning and development *versus* children setting their own standards. Teachers resolved such issues in complex ways which attempted to combine the 'best' of both poles of the dilemma. Thus, for example, in respect of teacher versus child decision making, Mrs Lawton resolved the dilemma by:

> making almost all of the decisions on *whether or not* and most of the decisions about *what*, *when*, and *how* in the basics — reading writing and maths — while leaving most decisions in the nonbasics to the children. 'I direct them, but I give them choice as well.' (p. 91)

Regarding types of motivation, Mr. Thomas attempted to evoke and use the interests of the children in all areas of the curriculum, but he did not depend solely on them: ' "If they are not interested in what they are doing, if I can't interest them in what they are doing then it becomes a case of having to do it." ' (p. 93). Mrs Lawton generally set standards of work, especially in academic subjects, for most children but not all: those pupils who could measure up to the teacher's standards without intervention were allowed to do so. Thus a much more complicated picture of the reality of teaching and learning in progressive classrooms is suggested by the writers, one which is not easily fitted into the stereotypes provided by protagonists or antagonists of progressive practices.

Clearly, schools change; primary schools are dynamic institutions which evolve, and practices modify over time. But the evidence consistently suggests that the kind of radical transformation of primary education that has been argued has occurred has not in fact done so. Thus it makes little sense to regard primary schools in the UK as having adopted the practices and methods advocated by Plowden wholesale. Rather, change has been patchy, hesitant and sometimes reluctant in the majority of schools. Teachers appear to be slow to adopt organizational or pedagogical innovations, and sometimes even positively resist change (cf Whiteside, 1978).

The Effectiveness of Progressive Methods

The question of whether progressive methods are as effective as those of more traditional kinds is much less easy to answer definitively. As suggested earlier, opponents of progressive ideas and methods have argued that their introduction has led to declining educational standards, an assertion denied by their advocates. However, an initial problem is that what *count* as educational standards in primary schools, or more generally what *should* be the aims and purposes of primary education, may be a matter of dispute, in spite of the air of consensus often implied, especially in government statements (for example, DES, 1978). For example, Plowden-style teachers may lay stress on *different* aims (for example initiative, critical thinking, the ability to express ideas and opinions, the ability to pursue tasks alone, etc.) from those of teachers using more traditional methods and it may be difficult to devise tests which measure to what extent pupils have attained such goals. Further, there is evidence that teachers (let alone the general public, parents, and so on) hold a huge variety of different aims for primary education, and success or failure in achieving very few of them has been assessed by empirical research. Bearing these cautions in mind, we can first look at a study of teachers' aims, and then at such research as is available concerning the relative effectiveness of different teaching styles in achieving them.

Teachers' Aims

Ashton *et al.* (1975) discussed the aims of primary education first with seven groups of teachers in the Midlands, and later with thirty-one further groups located in the West Country and in the North of England. Gradually, discussions were focussed and refined, but, nevertheless, the thirty-eight groups between them produced a vast number of aims which Ashton distilled to seventy-two. These aims were structured in terms of the aspect of development to which they referred, and in terms of the type of behavioural change desired among pupils, forming an eighteen cell matrix as follows:

	Desired behavioural change		
Aspect of development	*Knowledge*	*Skills*	*Qualities*
Intellectual			
Physical			
Aesthetic			
Spiritual/religious			
Emotional/personal			
Social/moral			

Source: Ashton *et al.*, (1975) *The Aims of Primary Education: A Study of Teachers' Opinions*, London, Macmillan, p. 15)

Examples of aims are: 'The child should have a wide vocabulary' (Knowledge–Intellectual), 'The child should be able to swim' (Skills–Physical) and 'The child should be industrious, persistent and conscientious' (Qualities–Social/moral). Some 1500 teachers from 200 primary schools of different types, sizes, areas, etc. were asked to rate each of the seventy-two aims on a five point scale: utmost importance, major importance, important, minor importance, no importance in primary education. No less than thirty-six aims on average were ranked as of utmost or major importance, which gives some indication of the sheer range of professional preoccupations of teachers. Equally interesting was the fact that of the eight aims generally regarded as most important of all, six were concerned with children's moral, social and personal development, such as 'the child should be happy, cheerful and well balanced' (ranked first) and 'the child should be beginning to acquire a set of moral values' (ranked third) and not with their actual academic progress (the two that were concerned reading). At the other extreme, large numbers of aims concerned with familiar areas of the usual curriculum of primary schools such as physical education, religious education, science, a second language, and all forms of the arts, did not appear among the top thirty-six aims, although the overwhelming majority of teachers thought *all* the aims were important to some degree. By 1979 when the survey was repeated (Ashton, 1981) with different teachers, and on this occasion only with teachers of 8 to 10 years old rather than the whole 5 to 11 age range as originally, there were some changes. Maths joined reading in the most important category, and intellectual aims in general were given somewhat increased stress, but overall the results were broadly similar, if slightly differently focussed: whether this is due to the different characteristics of the sample or to a real movement in teacher opinion is not clear.

Ashton (1981) also reports teachers' assessments of their own approach to teaching, again in terms of a five point scale: most traditional/traditional/moderate/progressive/most progressive. By far the largest category was 'moderate' in the 1971 sample, with 45.6 per cent of the teachers, and 29.2 per cent and 25.2 per cent tended to the traditional or progressive wings respectively. By 1979, teachers' self assessments were skewed further towards the traditional (44.4 per cent) and away from the progressive (15.6 per cent) (pp. 33–4). Further, Ashton (1978) concludes that for the original sample of teachers:

> Aims to do with children being self-controlled, purposeful, socially acceptable, hard working and obedient were given more importance by very many teachers than aims to do with children being socially effective in a more independent way, being able to make their own decisions and form their own opinions. (p. 31)

Such opinions and assessments are not evidence about performance: they do not tell us what teachers do. But neither do they provide any basis for suggesting that primary school teachers commonly engage in dramatically progressive practices.

But the central point of Ashton's work for present purposes is that accusations of ineffectiveness in the teaching of so-called basic skills to some extent miss the point. Teachers in primary schools appear to regard the teaching of such skills as important, but by no means exclusively so (although clearly what teachers say they believe and what they actually do in the classroom may not be identical). Empirical studies which assess schools and classrooms in terms of the competence of pupils at reading and mathematics but ignore the huge range of teachers' other, including 'non-intellectual', concerns for pupils are thus likely to be limited accounts of the reality of primary schools. However, in the main, such accounts are all that is available, and it is to the consideration of one or two examples that we now turn.

The Effects of Teaching Styles

The work of Start and Wells (1972) on the trend of reading standards suggested that reading attainment had risen between the end of the war and about 1964, but had then levelled out and according to one test, declined. The data are both complex and to some extent ambiguous, and the researchers themselves point to limitations in their work which, they suggest, necessitate caution. Nevertheless, the findings were largely taken as confirming what Black Paper and other critics had alleged, that standards were falling (for example, Boyson, 1975, pp. 6–7: Froome, 1975, pp. 9–13).

But, apart from Tyndale, the most significant event of the mid-1970s in relation to the work of primary schools was the publication in 1976 of Bennett's *Teaching Styles and Pupil Progress*. Although a relatively sophisticated academic research study, this suddenly achieved headline status in the press; in an important sense Bennett's work happened to be in the right place at the right time, because it lent itself to interpretations such as that of the *Daily Telegraph:* 'Old fashioned teaching is best ... Children taught by traditional classroom methods do far better at school than those taught in a modern, "progressive" way' (26 April 1976). Here then apparently was the 'hard', respectable evidence required: it had now been proved by research that progressive methods did not work (Cox and Boyson, 1977, pp. 12–13).

Bennett sent a questionnaire to the third and fourth year junior teachers in all 871 schools in Lancashire and Cumbria asking for biographical details, information on classroom organization, etc., as well as asking about testing, marking and discipline, and about the teacher's views on aims and methods. From the responses he received Bennett created a typology of twelve different teaching styles which for subsequent investigation were simplified into three — formal, mixed and informal. Formal teaching styles were characterized by (i) teaching separate subjects; (ii) restrictions on pupils' movement and talk in class; (iii) average or high amount of use of tests and grading; (iv) frequent talk by teacher to the whole class; (v) little or no pupil choice of work. Informal teaching had different characteristics: (i) integrated subject matter, (ii) relatively free pupil movement and talk in class; (iii) little use of tests or grading; (iv) average or low amount of teacher talk to the whole class; and (v) some pupil choice of work. The mixed style was in between on such characteristics, but the details of this style are not so significant since the main interest is in the contrast between formal and informal styles. After checking the accuracy of his categorizations by classroom observation by research staff and advisers from the local authority, Bennett selected thirty-seven teachers and classes for more detailed analysis in the second stage of the research. Twelve of these teachers were classified as formal, twelve as mixed, and thirteen as informal, and between them they taught some 1200 children, approximately equally divided between teachers of different styles. In June 1973 Bennett administered tests of reading, mathematics and English to the children at the end of their third junior year, and again in June 1974 at the end of their fourth year. They also completed personality tests at the beginning and end of the fourth year, and wrote descriptive and imaginative passages for analysis. About a hundred children were observed at work in the classroom using a recording schedule for this purpose.

Bennett found that pupils taught by teachers using formal styles demonstrated greater progress than those taught using informal styles in reading, mathematics and English and, except for reading, greater progress than those taught by mixed methods. Formally-taught pupils were also better at punctuation and much the same at spelling and story writing. In informal classrooms children were more motivated, but also more anxious; pupils in formal classrooms also spent more of their time actually working than did pupils in classes taught informally. However, Bennett also presents evidence that the 'best' teacher of all, i.e. the one whose pupils made most progress, was in fact one using informal styles.

Clearly it was not entirely Bennett's fault that his work was taken up and used as a nail in the coffin of progressive methods (indeed, the Co-director of the project specifically cautions against such interpretations in his foreword [1976, pp. ix–x]). However, largely because it was so used, the study attracted a great deal of academic as well as popular attention, and a great deal of criticism has been published. It is perhaps worth remembering that all educational research, given the complexity of the issues, has limitations; in all such work there are likely to be mistakes both of fact and of interpretation. Whether such limitations and errors are marginal to the conclusions of the study, or so fundamental that it must be doubted whether the central findings are valid, is often difficult to judge. In Bennett's case the criticisms are so numerous and substantial that they do seem to indicate that his findings are highly questionable.

Firstly, there are problems of sampling. Only thirty-seven teachers were involved in the second part of the study, and of these only thirteen and twelve adopted informal and formal styles respectively. Whether such a small number can be taken as representative is doubtful. It is, further, unclear to what extent Lancashire and Cumbria are typical areas. Secondly, it is difficult to be sure that it was teachers' style that was affecting pupils' attainment, rather than any one or more of a range of other factors. Wright (1977) suggests six possible influences which may have been important but which were not considered by Bennett:

> (a) the personal background of the pupils; (b) the quality of the home backgrounds, and parental attitudes; (c) the social class of the pupils; (d) the quality of the schools; (e) the quality of the teachers, including their length of experience and competence; (f) the *methods* of teaching reading employed, and the type of maths course followed. Any one of these factors could have been important enough to obliterate any difference the teaching style might have made. (p. 42)

Thirdly, there is a strong possibility that children in formal classrooms may have been more familiar with the styles of paper and pencil test used, particularly as many of them were in schools in areas where they had to engage in 11+ tests (of a rather similar kind) before transfer to secondary school. Fourthly, Bennett himself tends to exaggerate the statistical and educational significance of his results: evidence favourable to formal styles of teaching is emphasized and underlined; evidence favourable to informal styles is ignored or played down. Fifthly, Gray and Satterley (1976) made a number of technical criticisms of the statistical techniques, research design and sampling, which at the time Bennett refuted (Bennett and Entwistle, 1977). However, more recently he has substantially accepted such criticisms (Aitken, Bennett and Hesketh, 1981), saying that the statistical techniques available at the time the study was in progress were less effective than ones now available. Using the new techniques on the same data he finds that the differences between teachers was far greater than the differences between styles; in other words, there were effective and ineffective teachers using both formal and informal styles. Further, differences between styles were much smaller than he had previously thought and where there were differences these did not consistently favour formal styles. Finally, there is the anomalous case of the excellent informal teacher. If in fact it is style that is crucial, this teacher's pupils' progress is quite inexplicable. Once again, this case suggests that there are other factors which can override the influence of teaching style.

However, a more general problem with Bennett's work and much similar research is the categorization of teachers into a very small number of types or styles. In Bennett's case, while he began with twelve styles (and criticizes other research for using only two or three) these were in fact collapsed into only three for a substantial part of the research. The reasons for this are easy to understand: it is an extremely complex business to compare a relatively small number of teachers, divided simply two or three ways, on a small number of variables. To compare a larger number of teachers divided more subtly or into a greater set of types over a wider range of variables would make research unmanageable in view of the time, money and resources normally available. Nevertheless, it has to be questioned whether it makes much sense to divide the huge range of ideas, methods, styles, practices, beliefs and strategies of teachers into only two or three mutually exclusive types, whether they be formal, mixed and informal as in Bennett, or any of the multiplicity of dichotomies used by other writers and researchers. While such terms represent a useful starting point for discussion, ones which indicate in a very broad sense sets of approaches to primary education, they are inadequate for more detailed analysis. To take only one example, as Dale (1979, p. 195) has noted, it is absurd to apply the same label of 'progressive' to such diverse figures as Lady Plowden, John Holt, Terry Ellis and Henry Pluckrose, whose differences would seem to be at least as great as their similarities. Further, as has been argued by Hammersley (1977, p. 15), such terms are often used as 'thinly disguised labels for "good" and "bad"', as indeed can be seen in the debate following Plowden.

More complex categorizations have thus begun to be developed, such as Hammersley's proposal of four teaching paradigms: discipline-based, progressive, programmed and radical non-interventionist (1977, pp. 38–41), and Nash's five headteacher styles (1980, pp 63–5). One particularly relevant to the issue of the effectiveness of different teaching styles, however, is that developed by the 'ORACLE' researchers (Galton and Simon, 1980).

The 'ORACLE' Project

As stated earlier, these studies were based on observation of pupils and teachers rather than mainly on questionnaires and paper and pencil tests, although these were also used. Teachers were systematically observed for some eighteen hours a year each, and the main focus of attention was on their interaction with pupils. Eight children in each class, representing a balance of sexes and abilities were also closely observed. All the pupils were given tests of maths, reading and language use, and tests of 'study skills' designed to discover and record their attainments in interpreting block graphs, mapping and sequencing a story told in sounds. Pupils' abilities to listen with concentration and understanding, and to acquire information other than by reading were also assessed. Teachers were categorized by cluster analysis of the Teacher Records into six types, as follows:

(i) *Individual monitors* (22.4 per cent of the sample).
These teachers had the highest level of one-to-one interaction with pupils, but the lowest level of interaction with groups or with the whole class. Teaching was didactic and questioning was factual rather than open-ended. Pupils work was individualized and the teacher spent a lot of time monitoring pupils and marking their work.

(ii) *Class enquirers* (15.5 per cent of sample).
These teachers devoted the highest proportion of their time to whole class teaching and the least (although still a substantial amount) to individual interaction. Little time was spent interacting with groups. Such teachers used questioning a great deal and laid a relatively great emphasis on problem solving and the consideration of ideas.

(iii) *Group instructors* (12.1 per cent of sample).
These teachers worked with groups more than any other style, although still for only a fifth of the time. Teaching was mainly didactic, although such teachers made some attempts to involve children in problem solving; they provided a lot of feedback to pupils.

(iv) *Style changers* (50 per cent of sample).
Three rather different styles, all of whom tended to vary teaching strategies according to circumstances:

(a) *Infrequent changers* (10.3 per cent of sample).
These teachers occasionally and deliberately changed their teaching style according to the needs of particular classes of children. This group exhibited the highest level of questioning, especially open-ended and probing questions. Such teachers gave both ideas and feedback to the children and had the highest rate of interaction with pupils of all groups.

(b) *Rotating changers* (15.5 per cent of sample).
Pupils were grouped and each group worked in a different curriculum area. Groups rotated periodically by shifting physically from one table to another. Teachers showed a high degree of interaction related to supervision and control and spent a relatively large amount of time dealing with discipline problems.

(c) *Habitual changers* (24.2 per cent of sample).
Teachers varied their focus of instruction from the whole class to individuals according to their perceptions of the behavior of the children, both regularly and rather unpredictably. Relatively little time was spent on the use of questioning, especially open-ended questions, or the statement of ideas. This group spent least time in interaction with pupils.

The results of the tests undertaken by pupils were as follows: individual monitors' children did well at reading but badly on the maths and language skills tests; they also did badly at mapping and posing questions but well at block graphs and original drawings. Class enquirers' pupils made most progress of all on the maths and language tests but were relatively weak on reading progress. Children taught by such methods were good at posing questions but did less well at mapping and interpreting block graphs, and scored low on tests of originality. Children taught by group instructors made good progress in language, but not so much in reading and maths. These pupils did well at listening and acquiring information other than by reading.
    The infrequent changers' pupils did best of all at reading and well at maths, language and mapping, but less well in other areas. The pupils of habitual changers did rather badly at all the tests of basic skills, but best of all at the study skills, especially interpreting block graphs, mapping, and sequencing a story told in sounds. Finally, the rotating changers' pupils did very poorly in all the tests except one and even at that were not particularly successful.
    In summary, in the basic reading, mathematics and language skills the infrequent changers and the class enquirers seemed to be most effective, although the class enquirers did significantly less well at reading than styles stressing more individualized work, such as the individual monitors. In tests of the study skills it was the habitual changers' pupils who made most progress, followed by the class enquirers and the individual monitors. The only style which overall had practically nothing to commend it was that of the rotating changers.

Finally, the researchers looked for common patterns among eleven very successful teachers who between them used the three most effective basic skill styles; these teachers had several characteristics in common: they insisted on quietness in the classroom and interacted with the children for a very high proportion of the time. Organization and routine management was efficient and these teachers spent less time reminding children of instructions, thus freeing more time for explaining ideas, asking interesting questions, giving the children feedback, and encouraging them to solve problems for themselves.

Once again various criticisms are possible: the influence of being observed on teachers (the 'Hawthorne' effect) is difficult to assess; the tests and sampling procedures are open to criticism; tests once more measure only that which is easily measurable; not all the possible alternative explanations for the results were considered; is fifty-eight teachers sufficient upon which to generalize? However, this is a methodologically sophisticated and generally convincing account to which this brutally selective summary does not do justice. In particular it is of value in demonstrating that the apparently simple question of what is the most effective teaching style is not easy to answer. Stereotypes of progressive and traditional do not in any sense encompass the range of strategies and styles that teachers use: there is no one best buy. Effectiveness in teaching, at least in terms of the skills studied, may be achieved by the use of a variety of methods.

Conclusion

At this point some more general questions need to be raised about the strengths and weaknesses of the styles of research and kinds of evidence that have been considered in this chapter. While they are useful in providing a relatively objective and presumably reliable account of some aspects of primary schools, it is difficult to understand or explain from these studies *why* teachers and pupils engage in the practices described; we can note, for example, that teachers have not adopted innovations advocated by Plowden but we can find few clues as to the social processes involved in teachers' resistance. In the words of Cain and Finch (1981, p. 107) then, such material is to a large extent 'sociologically inert', static, untheorized and sometimes anaemic accounts of practice. Three reasons for this may be suggested: first, such styles of research purport to be value-free, in opposition to the blatantly ideological assertions of much prescriptive writing in education. Let us, such researchers implicitly say, cast aside all our preconceptions, opinions and beliefs, and with all the methodological rigour we can muster examine how it really is, without fear or favour. Let us, in other words, enter the primary school with, as it were, a blank mind and a blank sheet of paper, and let us record impartially and objectively what happens. But such a project is in fact impossible, because one cannot enter any social situation without pre-existing assumptions of some kind; in this case taking for granted what counts as an educational activity for example. How else would one know what to record and what to ignore? It would be impossible to record *everything* that happens, nor could one decide what is significant and what irrelevant without such assumptions. Thus no situation that is observed can be unproblematically reduced to data without interpretation (this applies with equal force to studies conducted via questionnaires). Take, for example, this fragment of conversation recorded in a classroom by Walker and Adelman (1976, p. 135):

> *Teacher:* Wilson we'll have to put you away if you don't change your ways and do your homework. Is that all you've done?
> *Pupils:* Strawberries, strawberries.

As it stands this is quite unintelligible; only when it is known that this teacher often comments that pupils' work is like strawberries (good as far as it goes, but doesn't last long enough) can this make sense — only by interpreting such an event in terms of some framework of understanding can it be made meaningful and thus appropriated as evidence.

Secondly, because it is impossible to approach the task of data-collection without assumptions — i.e. at least an implicit theory — a problem in the work that has been discussed earlier is that because such assumptions are subterranean and never made explicit, it is very easy for the reader to imbibe them without even being aware of their existence; and in the case of much of this research the implicit theory is educationally conservative. Take, for example, three different definitions of reading from the *Bullock Report* (DES, 1975) which are quoted and discussed by Berlak and Berlak (1981, pp. 265–7):

> *Definition A.* One can read in so far as he can respond to the language skills represented by graphic shapes as fully as he has learned to respond to the same language signals of his code represented by patterns of auditory shapes.

This is clearly a definition stressing the straightforward decoding of print. Definition B however lays emphasis on the reconstruction of the author's meaning, which the reader can demonstrate by summarizing his reading accurately:

> *Definition B.* The purpose of reading is the reconstruction of meaning. Meaning is not in print, but is meaning that the author begins with when he writes. Somehow the reader strives to reconstruct this meaning as he reads.

Definition C is different again. Rather than passively decoding or reconstructing the author's meaning, this definition requires the reader to actively and critically relate that meaning to the reader's experience:

> *Definition C.* A good reader understands not only the meanings of a passage, but its related meanings as well, which includes all the reader knows that enriches or illuminates the literal meaning. Such knowledge may have been aquired through direct experience, through wide reading or through listening to others.

Compare these definitions with Galton and Simon's (1980) account of the reading tests used in their research:

> The items in the reading test are taken from the Richmond Tests of Vocabulary and reading comprehension. The first half of the test consists of thirteen vocabulary items in which the pupil has to identify the synonym for a word from a list of four other words. The remainder of the test consists of short passages followed by questions testing comprehension, and the pupils have to identify the correct answer. (p. 47)

Clearly the definition of reading encompassed by the first half of the Richmond Tests is A, and of the second half B. Thus such tests exclude reading attainment in terms of an active and critical process by definition. The Berlaks (1981) conclude:

> If one accepts as an imperfect but nevertheless adequate measure of students' reading ability their performance on reading tests then one has, in effect, tacitly accepted as adequate the underlying definition of reading literacy that is built into the tests, a passive conception of the reading process. (p. 266)

In other styles of research that we have considered, such as that of the Inspectors' report on the state of primary education (DES, 1978; SED, 1980; DENI, 1981), the assumptions underlying the surveys and the criteria of evaluation used are not so much ignored as being irrelevant as assumed to be shared by all right-thinking citizens. For example, HMIs in England discussing the curriculum point to the 'deficiencies' in the teaching of science which their survey revealed (pp 58–63); they then assert the need for more and better teaching of the subject, as if the reasons for such changes are too obvious to require discussion. But they are not: perhaps there are good reasons why primary school teachers don't teach much science; why should it be taught at all (and not, say, economics)? The curriculum is not predetermined and unchallengeable, but is socially constructed and thus requiring critical analysis (see also Kelly, 1981).

Thirdly, in the terms used by Young (1971) in criticizing previous work in the sociology of education, such research 'takes' educator's problems (for example, how to teach children to read more effectively, how to achieve passes in eaminations) as constituting the only problems worth debate, rather than the researcher/sociologist engaging in a process whereby he 'makes' problems which may not be identical with those of practitioners. For example, the assumption that schools engage, more or less effectively, in practices whereby the education of young children is achieved is a deeply-rooted and taken-for-granted assumption in the research we have considered; in consequence it is implicitly assumed that such ideas represent also the values of *teachers* — but this is never demonstrated. Such an assumption thus systematically defines as irrelevant practices which achieve other goals (such as a teacher's overriding ambition to achieve promotion, or alternatively his concern for a pleasant and undemanding life); and defines as unproblematically consensual the meaning of what it is to be educated; in fact once again such ideas and practices are socially constructed and thus require analysis.

This is not to suggest that the studies discussed in this chapter are worthless, or that such problems are easily overcome, or that quantitative methods are necessarily inadequate (similar criticisms could be levelled at some ethnographic work) but to argue that research which neglects such issues is of doubtful value in terms of *understanding* the processes of primary education.

Summary

Evidence for a dramatic transformation of primary education in the last twenty years or so is hard to find. Both the organization of schools and classrooms and the practices of teachers within classrooms appear to have changed, but rather slowly and inconsistently; the evidence suggests evolution not revolution. It is almost certainly not true, then, that massive and fundamental changes have occurred or are occurring in primary education. Even schools which proudly proclaim their progressivism may not, in fact, fit the polarized stereotypes of much educational debate.

If such evidence is quite unambiguous, the same cannot be said about the many studies which have attempted to assess the effectiveness of different teaching styles. What is measured, and how, seem fundamental, and there is room for legitimate disagreement about both. While Bennett's work suggested that what he called formal styles were superior in terms of pupil attainment, this conclusion has been convincingly challenged by many critics. The more thorough and sophisticated ORACLE research suggested both that teachers employ a multiplicity of styles and that almost all had advantages and disadvantages in terms of effectiveness.

While such work is of interest in providing an intricately detailed picture of practice in primary schools and classrooms, it has been argued that its relative methodological sophistication may conceal an absent or inadequate theoretical foundation; such studies do not, in other words, comprise a *sociological* account of primary education. It is time to look at some work which does attempt to integrate theory and practice: it will form the substance of chapter 5.

5   Teachers, Pupils and Classroom Interaction

In the last fifteen years classroom processes and concomitantly participants in classrooms have been subject to increasingly close sociological examination and analysis. Previously, in spite of the pioneering work of Waller (1932) and with the exception of studies such as those of Becker (1952 and 1953) few ethnographic studies of schools were published, probably because the sociological paradigm of the time was not conducive to such work (Barton and Walker, 1978). However, the publication of research such as that of Jackson (1968) in America and by Hargreaves (1967) and Lacey (1970) in Britain was in part responsible for greater interest in school and classroom studies and the production of a wider range of material. As such work has proliferated, although it has mainly focused on secondary rather than primary schools, it has become increasingly clear that relatively simple conceptualizations of teachers, pupils and their interaction such as are inherent in many of the studies discussed in chapter 4 are unlikely to be adequate: classrooms are very complicated places and no fully satisfactory or comprehensive theory yet exists. For this reason this chapter will consist more of the indication of areas of uncertainty, problems yet to be analyzed let alone solved, and initial attempts at grappling with difficult issues, rather than definitive and conclusive answers.

Teachers

What do teachers bring to the classroom? What features of biography or social circumstance are significant for their work? What are their ideologies of education and on teaching? A number of studies have addressed these questions, of which the work of Jackson (1968) and Lortie (1975) are good examples.

Intuitive Teachers?

Jackson interviewed fifty teachers regarded as outstanding by administrators, assuming that such individuals, if not typical of all teachers, would be likely to be regarded as a model for others and thus influential within schools. Jackson describes four themes emerging from teachers' discourse: *immediacy* — a stress on the here and now urgency of classroom events: *informality* — less formal and rigid teaching styles and a more casual exercise of authority; *autonomy* — the perception and importance of freedom to teach spontaneously; and *individuality* — a focus on, and interest in, individual pupils. Jackson proceeds to draw out three main implications. First, he argues that teachers lack a technical vocabulary and talk in conceptually simple terms: teachers have an uncomplicated view of causality, a ready acceptance of apparent 'miracles', an intuitive approach to classroom events, a committed stance to the practice of teaching and a narrowness of working definitions. For example, action is based on feelings rather than rationally thought-out procedures and ad hocing and ad libbing is frequent. Secondly, the 'sharp existential boundaries' (1968; p. 147) of teaching, the fact that teachers are firmly embedded in the 'blooming, buzzing confusion' (1971, p. 33) leads to an intense emotional involvement with pupils. Thirdly, Jackson discerns an attitude of acceptance of the organizational context in which the teacher works, a lack of interest in change, and an acceptance of the educational status quo.

Jackson sums up his interviewees' attitudes as 'tinged with a quasi-mystical faith in human perfectibility' (1968, p. 150) yet argues that this and the other qualities he describes 'have adaptive significance' (p. 149) i.e. enable teachers to cope successfully with the demands of classroom life, in contrast to, say, a more reflective, open-minded, rational or dispassionate approach, which he suggests would lead to chaos.

The source of these teacher perspectives lies then essentially in experience, the press of reality, the speed, complexity, uncertainty and concreteness of classrooms. The stress of professional socialization on 'oughtness' contrasts markedly with the 'isness' of classrooms.

Conservative Teachers?

Lortie (1975) in a large scale and complex interview-based study, argues firstly that classroom teachers (mainly women) are recruited from those who positively identify with schools as they are and that because teaching is personal and idiosyncratic, professional socialization and experience (in isolation) does little to alter such initially conservative orientations. Secondly, the career-structure of teaching by which promotion removes skilled practitioners (especially men) from classrooms and provides few extrinsic rewards for skilled practice leads to a perspective stressing the present; the future, for most classroom teachers, is likely to be similar to here and now, so there is little need to defer gratification. Thirdly, and partly in consequence the rewards of teaching are seen as individual and intrinsic, the psychic fulfilment associated with successful relationships with and instruction of pupils, even though the 'endemic uncertainties' of the classroom, the lack of a technical culture to resolve problems, the perception of learning as a hit or miss affair, the lack of career lines and the isolation may lead to a 'diffuse anxiety'.

Teachers regard the classroom and classroom events as of crucial relevance: other contexts (for example, school organization) are of lesser importance. Thus teachers resent obstacles, interruptions, lack of support, and constraints of time or space which disturb or prevent concentration on classroom teaching. However, Lortie detects an ambivalence: the desire for independence and more resources yet the willingness to concede control and power to others outside the classroom (notably the head).

Finally, interpersonal expectations of parents, colleagues and headteachers fit with the teacher's commitments to classroom-centred rewards: the desire for autonomy and yet for support, the acceptance of authority in the interests of overcoming constraints. The way in which teachers view tasks is reinforced by their view of the way things were done in the past; ambiguous criteria of effectiveness and the structure of careers and classrooms lead them to make individual choices and to resist change.

Child-Centred Teachers?

The influence of work like that of Jackson and Lortie is perceptible in recent British studies of teachers' perspectives. Sharp and Green (1975), for example, viewed the infants' class teachers they studied at Mapledene, a self-consciously innovative primary school on a London housing estate in the early 1970s, as having adopted more or less consistently a radical rhetoric of child-centredness, an anti-authoritarian and anti-idealist perspective in which the child's 'needs', 'readiness' and 'choice' were paramount. The children would learn what was appropriate for them as individuals at whatever stage they were, by a process of discovery. At the same time the failure of some children to achieve was explained by appealing to the idea that the most the school could do was to provide a supportive and therapeutic context in which such children could 'work through' their problems, problems which arose from their 'deprivation' at home. This social-pathological view of children's home background is one which pervaded teachers' discourse and thinking; the headmaster's perspective, for example, involved a:

> fusion of, on the one hand, a child-centred perspective towards education, whilst, on the other, a social pathology view of the community from which his pupils are drawn. He sees the school as dealing with seriously deprived children who are both emotionally and cognitively underdeveloped and thus the school has to provide a socializing environment, or as he puts it 'a civilizing force' which can secure a supportive context in which the children can develop. (p. 62)

Similarly, King (1978) who based his research on observation of and discussion with thirty-eight infants' school teachers in three schools, suggests that teachers adopted both child-centred and social pathology perspectives (the latter he calls 'family-home background theory').

Teachers' ideologies were child-centred, stressing the development and individualism of children, play as a learning process and the 'innocence' of childhood. Teachers had clear notions of children's sequential change, physically, emotionally and intellectually; of the importance of suiting approaches to the individual child's putative needs; a view of play as a natural and significant aspect of learning; and a concept of childish innocence: children could not be held responsible as they were not seen as morally in control of their actions. These ground-rules were used in combination, in differing degrees and according to different circumstances. King suggests, for example, that if children changed in ways which teachers approved, such changes were regarded as part of natural development. If, however, children changed for the worse in teachers' eyes, then explanations were sought in factors external to the 'innocent' child, such as illness or problems at home. This 'family-home background' theory was of particular importance as a means of explaining discrepancies between self-concept as a good teacher, the presumed characteristics of children, and children's behaviour and attainments which were apparently incompatible with such concepts and characteristics. Similarly, following the idea of innocence, oblique forms of social control were used, such as those dependent on the idea that age (development) led to greater maturity and thus the expectation of more 'sensible' behaviour:

> Terry, why did you walk after I said stop? You are one of the biggest in the class and you know you should stop. Tracey, you moved, but you are new (Teacher to pupils in PE, p. 56).

Again, teachers held collective views of appropriate styles of relationship with children: pleasantness (a deliberate and public 'niceness' signalled by posture, voice and movement); affection (again a deliberate and controlled expression of liking) and equanimity (a calm and unemotional, distanced response to classroom disasters which in children's innocence could not be blamed on them). The good teacher, as well as these essential characteristics, was administratively efficient, put on good public performances both personally and through 'her' children, and her classroom was busy with activity. Deviant teachers lacked one or more of these characteristics, rejecting the child-centred ideology explicitly or implicitly.

Uncertain Teachers?

Implicit in these studies is the idea that a major problem for teachers is the fact that their job is so diffuse, lacking any clear criteria whereby they can measure their success or failure in the task of socializing children or even in that of transmitting skills and knowledge (Wilson, 1962). For this reason, although teachers may regard themselves as experts in pedagogy, such expertise is held insecurely and defensively, because teachers are in fact uncertain as to how or if pedagogical goals are achieved. Goals are opaque: teachers may often have to work for long periods without much feedback as to whether or not their efforts are successful. Because it is difficult for any individual to continue to work not knowing whether or not she is achieving very much, teachers tend to replace the ultimate educational goals with ones that are more proximate, immediate and attainable, and more easily related to the techniques that they are using. Some evidence for this process can be found in a study of the perspectives of forty-five teachers in three junior schools ('Village', 'Estate' and 'City') that I undertook (1981). Among the teachers a common worry was the absence of criteria for assessment of their work; this theme often emerged in discussion of the fact that the 11+ examination, although disliked in many ways, had in earlier years provided some means of evaluation:

> I don't know whether they'll bring back the 11+ or anything, I didn't like it but it did give us a goal to achieve. (City school)

> I don't know what I'm aiming for — the 11+ at least was a target, at least it set some sort of standard of performance whereas nowadays (teachers) drift along without any real aim about what way we're trying to go or what we're trying to achieve. (Village school)

Because long-term goals were cloudy and difficult, teachers tended to replace them with short-term measures of success. One example was teachers' emphasis on the achievement of demonstrable pupil competence in some limited and circumscribed areas of the curriculum, often referred to as the 'basics'. In practice, basics consisted of structured facts and skills in English (grammar, spelling, punctuation and 'comprehension') and mathematics (tables, simple arithmetical operations) which had, at all costs, to be inserted into children. Many teachers made comments like:

> I feel my job as a primary teacher which I feel very strongly about is to put the basics into these children. (City school)

While teachers generally stressed the 'basics' because it was taken for granted that they were essential to the future academic success of pupils, they were also aware of their utility from the teacher's point of view:

> if the children produce reasonable type of written work or they're reasonably well-behaved or they seem to be getting something out of it then you can justify it . . . you know you want to have the satisfaction of being able to see some results, some concrete results. (Estate school)

Another example of a short-term objective, also used by teachers as a substitute for longer term goals, and also regarded by them as of central significance was the maintenance of order. In the three schools I studied there were two important reasons why teachers regarded control as vital: first, it was argued that without such control children could not learn. Control and teaching and learning were inextricable; as one suggested in interview, order was:

almost axiomatic. I couldn't teach, I don't think anyone can teach without reasonable discipline; you've got to know that the children in your class are working. (Estate school)

Secondly, control was essential because teachers were isolated for long periods of time in their work. They thus had few opportunities to make informed judgements of colleagues' work. Nevertheless, teachers did assess their peers, usually on the relatively visible criterion of order (for example, movement of class around the school, noise emanating from classrooms, and impressions on brief visits) and most wished to be regarded by colleagues, and by the headteacher in particular, as competent and successful. Thus, as one teacher perceptively noted:

> I think the area I become obsessed with most is noise because I feel if my class is making a hell of a row that people passing by and other teachers will think that my God, his class is making a hell of a row, and I want them quiet, but I sometimes from time to time wake up to the realization that I don't want quiet for itself but I want it quiet because I feel that I will be criticized if I have a noisy class. (Estate school)

Control, then, was an important indicator of success; teachers believed that learning could not occur in the absence of order and that well behaved pupils were one appropriate indicator to peers that the teacher was competent. For many teachers, as McPherson (1972) has noted:

> having assumed that disorder prevented learning, the teacher went on to assume that by producing order she had brought about learning. (p. 34)

While teachers' emphasis on the 'basics' was justified by reference to the requirements of society for literate and numerate citizens, their stress on order was legitimated in a more complex way. Two themes pervaded teachers' discourse in this area, which may be called 'domino theory' (Lacey, 1976) and 'decline and fall'. Domino theory suggested that chaos and anarchy would result unless vigilance was maintained. Any weakness or chink in teachers' defences and indiscipline would become increasingly inevitable and catastrophic; relaxation would lead irrevocably to the kind of chaos thought to have occurred at William Tyndale school. Teachers argued that one reason why disorder was an ever present threat was the nature of children; a head presented an almost Durkheimian thesis:

> I don't believe that children are naturally good. I work from
> that base. I think if they're left to their own devices, they
> wouldn't naturally be good, I think children have to be
> taught, they have to be encouraged and all the rest of it in
> order to at least keep up the standard of civilization which
> we've acquired. I can't quote it now, but someone said, what
> is it, teachers are faced with a horde of barbarians. (Village
> school)

A further reason for the tendency of disorder to overwhelm teachers
was the baleful influence of 'society'; teachers saw themselves as
struggling to counteract the effects of the media, especially 'rubbish
subculture from America', urban stress and the break up of the
nuclear family, low moral standards, problems caused by immigrant
children, and above all, 'the most pressing problem for schools is
counteracting home influence'. Thus, to take just one example:

> Parents are a lot more lax than they were. I think you can put
> it down initially to the parents and then schools find it
> difficult to control them. (Village school)

For such reasons then:

> You've got to be authoritarian to a certain extent. I think
> you've got to be; otherwise there's chaos particularly with
> these children who have little self-control at home and very
> little self-control. (Estate school)

But not only are social forces (media, urbanism, family problems)
bearing down on teachers with all but irresistible force, they are
doing so with increasing pressure, because in the (undated) past
social, moral and educational conditions were better than today and
since that high point decline has set in. For example:

> It's general life isn't it? We accept things now that we
> wouldn't have dreamed of accepting. It's just our whole life
> has gone right down. It's not just education, it's sort of right
> across. (City school)

While this 'decline and fall' had implications for all of teachers' work,
it was particularly significant in the context of order. Teachers saw
themselves, Canute-like, as battling against the tide:

> *Interviewer:* Your attitude is whatever the rest of the world
> is doing —
> *Teacher:* Whatever the rest of the world is doing, I still

think there is need for what I've said... These values are
permanent. (Village school)

Thus, because of the innate nature of children and because of dire
social, moral and educational conditions (which indeed are getting
worse) the maintenance of control is an unremitting and difficult
struggle.

In these three schools at least, then, teachers laid great stress on
pupil learning of 'basics' in a tightly ordered environment. Such
perspectives were justified by reference to (short-term) educational
goals, but also in terms of their usefulness in demonstrating teacher
competence. Underlying both were a set of implicit social and
political ideas which reinforced the pedagogical techniques the
teachers used.

Summary

It may be useful at this point to summarize some of the most
important aspects of these and other studies which have contributed
towards the understanding of teachers' perspectives, as follows:

(i)   Teachers are recruited from upper working or lower middle
      class backgrounds and have themselves succeeded in the tradi-
      tional education system. These facts may contribute to prob-
      lems which arise for them in dealing with children from other
      social classes, especially those for whom academic success is
      not a central goal.

(ii) Teachers tend to social and educational conservatism, partly
      because of patterns of recruitment, and partly because the
      nature of classroom routine leads to faith in (and regression to)
      'tried and trusted' approaches.

(iii) The immediacy and urgency of classroom events both disguises
      and reinforces a reluctance (or inability) of teachers to expose
      themselves to intellectual analysis of ends and means, and
      practice is instead analyzed in terms of 'experience', feeling and
      intuition; the emphasis on the uniqueness and individuality of
      children leads to the view that general or theoretical statements
      are inapplicable or irrelevant.

(iv) Teachers regard questions of ultimate goals as cloudy and
      difficult (because of the absence of clear evidence of their
      success or otherwise in achieving them) so short-term objec-
      tives, which can be specified fairly exactly, such as the main-

tenance of order or the skilled practice of the technical craft of teaching, tend to be substituted for long term goals.

(v)   Discipline and control are crucial contexts for the demonstration of competence both for the maintenance of the teacher's self-esteem, and for impressing significant others with skilled practice.

(vi) Teachers may value the intrinsic rewards of interpersonal relationships with children and their ability to control knowledge as much as or even more than extrinsic career or financial rewards. In consequence they resist threats to autonomy of classroom practice; external factors (such as authorities) are evaluated according to the extent to which they protect or threaten autonomy and whether they increase or ameliorate organizational constraints on teachers' work.

(vii) Teachers explain apparent failure not by locating 'deficiencies' in their ideology or practice but by blaming factors outside their control, notably the family and socio-cultural environment of the children, although as the child matures this is partly replaced by a tendency to 'blame the victim' viewing the child's innate incapacity as a basic cause.

Confused Teachers?

While in some respects the ideas and evidence incorporated in such studies contribute to a sensitive understanding of teachers, in other ways they are more contentious. A pervasive theme in such work is of the teacher as lacking in intellectual rigour, acting on the basis of feeling and intuition, or even as 'cultural dope'. Most primary school teachers are women, and feminist writers in particular have objected to the characterization of teachers as 'deficient, distracted, and sometimes even dim' (Acker, 1983, p. 124). One problem is that writers like Jackson and Lortie base their assessments of teachers on interviews, and never observed them or participated with them in classroom interaction and they thus provide no evidence as to how analytic, rational (or not) teachers are in actual practice. Further, it could be argued that the hypothetical and abstract questions typical of formal interviews are extremely difficult for anyone (not only teachers) to answer: teachers' understandings exist in the context of the classroom — when that context is removed, as in an interview setting, it is not surprising that they sometimes appear hesitant, confused or incoherent.

One study which usefully attempts to relate teachers' perspectives with their practice is that of A. and H. Berlak (1981). Their article on progressive practice was discussed earlier, but in their book they have developed much further their framework of analysis regarding the 'dilemmas' of schooling. The Berlaks describe their observations of classroom practice mainly in three schools over a period of six months in the early 1970s. They argue that simple dichotomies like progressive/traditional and the assumption of necessary causal connections between teachers' formally stated opinions or values and their actual practice can be very misleading. Rather, their reading of theoretical work rooted in the ideas of Mead and Marx leads them to explore teaching in terms of a 'language of acts' in which specific acts derive from a complex interplay of external and internal forces: the individual's biography and social experience, social and institutional constraints, but also his reflection on and interpretation of such pressures, interpretations which are themselves mediated by experience. The relation between the external and the internal is thus, the Berlaks suggest, a *dialectical* one: the individual is a 'potentially active agent, a person who is capable of processing external experience but is also limited by that experience' (1981, p. 131). The dilemmas of schooling, of which they suggest sixteen, focus on control (tensions over the degree and kind of control over pupils), curriculum (controversies over questions concerning the transmission of knowledge), and society (contradictions related to equality, justice, and relations between social, racial, age and sex groups of pupils). These dilemmas represent, they suggest, contradictory pulls and pushes on the teacher in his work. For example, the 'control' dilemmas consist of pressures on the teacher towards taking responsibility for the totality of children's development, or towards cognitive learning only; towards tight or little control of pupil behaviour, and of how pupils should engage with the curriculum; and towards teacher control of acceptable standards of work or towards encouraging children to be self-evaluative. While individuals adopt a 'dominant' or usual mode of resolution to such dilemmas, which obviously may vary from teacher to teacher, 'exceptional' resolutions may arise within situations which appear to an observer (but not to the actor) as identical. For example, Mr Scott believes that maths is a crucial aspect of the curriculum yet he allows two boys to spend their time discussing football cards. The apparent inconsistency occurs because Mr Scott is pushed and pulled towards alternate behaviours reflecting the horns of the dilemma of childhood unique *versus* childhood continuous (i.e. seeing childhood as a time in which life is to be lived for itself, *or* as a period of preparation for adulthood). Mr Scott's action is thus not arbitrary or confused but represents an occasion when he:

> asks himself whether, *in this particular set of circumstances*, he values getting ahead over allowing this child to share his excitement ... and for the first time resolves his competing tendencies to act in a way that appears discontinuous with his past behaviour (p. 131).

The Berlak's work is of great interest as portraying teachers as active and to some degree autonomous rather than as holders of rather static and reified perspectives; (cf Nias (1984), who describes some primary teachers' adoption of committed yet highly individualistic values). However, the evidence the Berlaks provide particularly in terms of the biographical, social and institutional constraints on teachers is often sketchy, and may be regarded more as illustrative of ways in which their framework of analysis could be used to understand teachers' practice rather than as a conclusive interpretation of primary schooling. A further problem with their work, one which they share with the other research discussed earlier, is the virtual absence of discussion of pupils, who are implicitly regarded as the raw material upon which teachers work. But pupils too are active and complex, and without some consideration of the perspectives of primary school children, such accounts are at best one-sided.

Pupils

Teachers are relatively easy to study, but pupils much less so. For one thing, teachers themselves may resist research into pupils' ideas about teachers and teaching on the grounds that:

> It is dangerous to involve children in this kind of comment on their teachers.
> Discipline would be adversely affected by this kind of exercise.
> It is bad for classroom relationships.
> Children are not competent to judge these matters. (Meighan, 1978, p. 105, quoting comments by headteachers).

Versions of the last comment have been seen as particularly important in respect of the perspectives of younger children: what after all, it has been suggested, is the validity or significance of the views of a six year old? Further, with a few exceptions (for example, School of Barbiana, 1970) education is written about *by* adults, notably teachers or ex-teachers, *for* adults, again mostly teachers. Implicit in the approach of most such writers is the idea that what really matters in schools is what teachers do to pupils, the ideals teachers have, the techniques they use, the problems they face, and so on. For this reason, as Calvert (1975) has suggested:

> Because the teacher thus defines the pupil role, he tends to see himself as the more decisive participant in the performance, and thinks of the pupil's role as more receptive than his own. Things are done by the teacher to or for the pupil, just as things are done by the doctor to or for his patient; and the pupil, like the patient, is expected to conform to the expectations thus set up for him. (p. 4).

However, a number of sociological writers have suggested that it is misleading to approach any organization in a way which views the perspectives and practices of people with officially defined power and responsibility (for example, doctors in hospitals, teachers in schools), as the only ones worth taking into account; rather, it has been argued that all participants affect the working of institutions and that therefore the perspectives of 'underdogs' cannot be omitted. For example, Goffman's (1968) study of a mental hospital is mostly written from the point of view of the patients, and he shows how while from the official standpoint the hospital was a place where people who were ill were treated and cared for and eventually returned to the outside world cured by medical science, from the patients' point of view the hospital appeared as a 'total' institution, one that set out to control every aspect of inmate's lives, and in which all patients' actions were subject to official scrutiny. From the patients' viewpoint such control appeared arbitrary, alienating and suffocating. Thus the official interpretation of the nature and purpose of the hospital contrasted markedly with the patients' view of an impersonal and rigid bureaucracy which, however, could often be subverted and outwitted. Thus Goffman's implicit argument is that if one suspends the assumption that 'underdogs' in organizations are unreliable, misinformed or simply unimportant, one can gain revealing insights into the nature of such organizations. Woods (1977b), among others, has developed this idea in the context of schools, and provides an imaginary example which neatly illustrates the idea that pupil perspectives are equally rational and logical to those of teachers once they are viewed from the pupils' side of the desk; first, the teacher's view of an event:

> A class comes into my room, and one of the boys calls out to me 'Happy Christmas'.
> I wonder for a moment whether he is being impertinent, or just friendly. I could cuff him round the ear, or smile and say 'Happy Christmas' back, The latter might help establish good rapport, and a relaxed, casual atmosphere. But my knowledge of the child (he doesn't like authority, and is always trying to bring teachers down a peg or two), others like him (always 'taking the mickey' to undermine the lessons so they need do no work), and the likely effect on others (respect for sequence) lead me to decide that it is cheek.
> I cuff him round the ear and say 'Don't be impertinent, boy!'
> He scowls, and goes to his desk in silence. I turn my attention to the class.

Now the same event viewed by the pupil:

> I feel happy today, it is near the end of term, nearly Christmas, the atmosphere is becoming casual, this teacher's not a bad sort, it is customary among my folk to show goodwill towards others and try to make them happy.
> I say 'Happy Christmas' to him. He cuffs me round the ear.
> I feel anger. It bring out in me all I detest in teachers.
> He's also made me look ridiculous in front of my friends. I resolve on revenge.
> As soon as his back it turned, I get busy with the pea-shooter, jew's harp and stink bombs.
> Teacher turns, clearly harassed, and shouts and threatens. I feel satisfied. (p. 27)

To understand schools, therefore, we have to attempt to take account of the perspectives of pupils, even though it is very difficult for us to see the world in the way that a 5 year old does. Its value, however, lies in the fact that behaviour that appears foolish or absurd or simply 'childish' may be shown to be quite consistent and thoughtful:

> I spent that first day picking holes in paper, then went home in a smouldering temper.
> 'What's the matter, Love? Didn't he like it at school, then?'
> 'They never gave me the present.'

'Present? What present?'

'They said they'd give me a present.'

'Well, now, I'm sure they didn't.'

'They did! They said: "You're Laurie Lee, aren't you? Well just you sit there for the present." I sat there all day but I never got it. I ain't going back there again.' (Lee, 1962, p. 44).

From the teacher's point of view little Laurie was no doubt being very silly, but he was in fact acting quite logically from within his understanding.

Pupils in School

There is some rather indirect evidence that primary school children generally like school (65 per cent of pupils according to Blishen, 1973, p. 255; and 55 per cent suggested by the Newsons, 1977, p. 26, although neither sample may be fully representative). What is apparent from accounts written by children is the thoughtfulness and keen observation which pupils bring to bear on their schools and teachers. Makins (1969a and b) and Blishen (1973) analyzed 1200 and 400 accounts written by pupils respectively, and their summaries of children's ideas of the characteristics of a good teacher are remarkably similar:

> Teachers who do not shout, teachers who let you talk, teachers who explain, teachers who encourage, teachers who are interested (Makins, 1969a, p. 22).

> Approval of kindness, a sense of humour, patience in explanation: disapproval of shouting, favouritism, boringness (Blishen, 1973, p. 256).

The sophistication of many of the children's perceptions is remarkable; a few examples from Makins' and Blishen's accounts may illustrate their quality:

> Well, she's only human. She does her best.

> There are some very bad teachers that nobody knows about except the children.

> When she was angry it may have been that she was angry inside or I was being naughty (or the opposite) this was fairly hard to tell as Miss Wolf I think kept covered up what she felt inside.

> She is really a good teacher but we hardly get any pleasure at
> all in our class.
>
> Instead of marking books the education authorities should
> provide a man to mark books.
>
> If the children do not show intelligence it is often the sign of a
> bad teacher.

There is also evidence of pupils' ability to penetrate stratifying
practices which are not usually overtly publicized by teachers. For
example, Nash (1973) reports on a non-streaming primary school in
Scotland where the children were extremely sensitive to their academic status vis a vis other pupils and he concludes that this sense of
position is a crucial accomplishment of schools: whatever else they do
or fail to do, schools teach a sense of hierarchical levels of personal
worth very successfully.

Thus while little research has been undertaken on the perspectives of primary school pupils on teachers and teaching it would be a
mistake to conclude either that pupils (even the youngest) have no
clear idea of what is happening in classrooms, no firm expectations of
and opinions about the process of schooling, or that such views are
irrelevant to the understanding of schools. But such ideas and
opinions about teachers and classroom practice are only a small part
of children's social experience in school. During their primary school
years they are introduced to a world much wider than that of the
family, and just as we saw earlier that teachers are well aware of the
social, moral and aesthetic dimensions of their work (Ashton, 1975)
so pupils too gradually discover and participate in a culture within
which the business of learning to read and write and so on are of
relatively minor concern. A number of sociologists have documented
the existence of this 'hidden curriculum' (for example, Jackson, 1968;
Eggleston, 1977; Hargreaves, 1977). An interesting example is provided by the Newsons (1977) in a study mainly concerned with
parents' perspectives on school and education, where they introduce
the idea that very young children are rapidly inducted by both peers
and by teachers into patterns of behaviour and understanding rather
different to those familiar at home. They suggest for example that:

> By witnessing small acts of deference, they sense that their
> own class teacher is considered less important than the
> headteacher . . . In the playground they notice who does the
> pushing around and who gets pushed; who always has a
> bosom friend or two and who has none; who are the rough

and noisy ones and always get told off. They are told that when you talk to Jesus you must shut your eyes, and when you go to the toilet you must shut the door ... They learn that telling tales isn't approved of, but there are ways of laying a complaint if you choose your words carefully ... And through repeated observation and personal involvement, they discover the values to which teachers and pupils subscribe in the world of school: what is regarded as especially clever or especially praiseworthy; what is considered babyish or mardy; where teacher-pupil values overlap, and where they separate or contradict each other (as in 'who can pee highest up the wall', an ability much prized by little boys but notably undervalued by teachers and dinner-ladies). (p. 42)

While this suggests a somewhat passive process of socialization into the informal culture of the school it has been shown, especially in the classic work of the Opies (1959) that children's culture is participated in much more actively than the Newsons imply. The Opies detail the immensely complex oral tradition of children — their rhymes and riddles, rules and rituals, jokes and games — and show that they are both rooted in the past (in the sense that many were known centuries ago and handed down from generation to generation) but also being changed creatively to fit topical events and personalities. For example, in the mid-1950s they recorded the incorporation of Mickey Mouse, Davy Crockett and various film stars, and more recently Sluckin (1981) has shown that the likes of Starsky and Hutch and Spiderman co-exist in Oxford playgrounds with the ancient Chinese game of 'paper scissors stone'.

Only in the last few years has the pioneering work of the Opies been followed up systematically, partly perhaps because there are particularly difficult methodological problems in studying children's cultures by means of interviews. Primary school children generally regard it as in their interests to please adults and it is possible that while the researcher may believe that he is asking open questions designed to discover what the pupil 'really' thinks about a particular issue, the child is sussing out what kind of answer will keep him or her happy. Thus, for example, an apparently open question such as 'what do you particularly like about school?' may well conceal the interviewer's implicit assumption that the answer will be focussed on subjects, teachers and academic learning; a reply such as 'eating crisps at playtime' may be regarded as flippant or irrelevant. The researcher's verbal or non-verbal reaction or even lack of encourage-ment of such a response may be taken by the pupil as a cue that his world, vital to him, is of no importance, and frame his answers accordingly. Such problems have made the generation of sensitive and appropriate research procedures very difficult but two recent studies have in different ways attempted to do so and thus get at the ways in which children both discover and invent a culture, both take it for granted and construct or reconstruct it.

Pupils in the Playground

The first, by Sluckin (1981) solved the problem by observing primary school pupils (who were only very loosely supervised by adults) in two Oxford playgrounds, but maintaining a policy of non-interaction with the children who, he suggests, soon came to regard him as part of the playground furniture and did not notice that he was observing and recording their words and actions. His work, like that of the Opies, points to the significance of the playground as a site in which children learn as or more effectively than in the classroom, but a different kind of learning; he shows how children's social experience at playtime is not anarchic and arbitrary but ordered and rule-bound. Children 'learn how to join a game, how to choose and avoid roles, how to deal with people who cheat and make trouble, and above all else how to manipulate situations to their advantage' (p. 119). For example, before a game can begin roles are often allocated by 'dipping', an apparently unambiguous and fair technique based on chance selection. However, many dips are complex and in practice provide endless opportunities for the interpretation of the rules (or more crudely, cheating) in order to gain or avoid a particular role — indeed, sometimes the game never gets going at all because of the length of time and amount of negotiation required:

> During the dip, Mukesh (5:9) has to say a number.
> *Arthur* (8:8):   Say a number straightaway.
> *Ramesh* (8:8):   Look at my finger. (He puts up one finger.)
> (Ramesh and Mukesh are brothers.)
> *Malcolm* (7:9):   Don't you dare say one.
> *Ramesh:*   Look at my finger, say a number.
> *Mukesh:*   Four.
> *Malcolm:*   That's not fair, you counted that.
> Ramesh, Malcolm, Arthur each have one foot left in; Mukesh

none. The count lands on Arthur.

Malcolm: You're not allowed to count.

Arthur: You're going to start (the count) with you (Malcolm)?

Malcolm: Don't you dare say three.

Arthur: Nine.

Malcolm: You cheat, you cheat, you cheat by thinking.

Arthur: I did not. (p. 52)

The implications of such processes (in this case all the boys are 'cheating', but Arthur most skilfully in that he can count ahead 'by thinking' instead of by counting aloud) are obviously important; Sluckin argues that in the playground children are constantly learning what behaviour is appropriate for different situations, acquiring new skills, and most important of all engaging with the concept of rules: how they are initiated, constituted, applied, bent and broken; and that these are all essential aspects of playground life viewed as a preparation for adulthood.

Davies (1982) tackled the same methodological problems as those faced by Sluckin by means of flexible conversations with groups of (Australian) primary school pupils which were not tied to the researcher's agenda but which explicitly set out to explore what issues were of central concern to the children. Similar themes to those of Sluckin emerge in this study (which suggests that at least some aspects of children's culture are transnational!) such as the centrality and constant exploration of rules which could be manipulated, manoeuvred around, and reconstructed to gain contingent advantages. Davies shows that children's concept of friendship (that is, the rules governing who is a friend such as the rule of reciprocity) is stable, but children appear to make and break friends with great rapidity only because adults do not generally understand how the rules of friendship are being applied. Such ruptures of friendship are in fact merely part of the process of manoeuvring that occurs *between* friends: looking for personal advantage, testing the limits of friendship, exploring the boundaries of the rules, and so on. Two girls discussed their relationship as follows:

Jane: Yes, we've got the same sort of personality I suppose (pause) we can be happy and mad at the same time, and we can change our ways in just a second.

Vanessa: We both seem to change at the same time.

Jane: We start squabbling at the same time and we always end at the same time.

> *B.D.:* So when you get mad at each other, do you not really
> get mad? Is it all part of a joke or are you really mad?
> *Vanessa:* Yes, it's sorta, bit of a joke, trying each other out.
> (pp. 81–2)

Davies suggests that such comments show that by squabbling they are exploring the boundaries of their friendship; by testing the limits of the rules they discover and rediscover what the rules are. She concludes that children require adults to be sensitive to the serious-ness of the culture of childhood and to the seriousness of their membership, which involves adherence to rules and participation in patterns of interaction different to those of adults' cultures.

Such studies as those of Sluckin and Davies are fascinating accounts of the perspectives of young children but also tentative and exploratory. Much subtle and sensitive research is needed before a more complete picture of the social world of children is available. At this point, however, we need to bring teachers and children together and look at their interaction in the classroom.

Interaction

A little earlier the study of the Berlaks was considered as an example of a relatively sophisticated approach to teachers and teachers' perspectives. The range of problems and issues they discussed have been analyzed within different conceptual frameworks by an increas-ingly large number of other writers interested in the interaction of teachers and pupils in classrooms (see Delamont, 1983 for an extended discussion of such work). Recently, such analyses have focussed on what the Berlaks called the 'mode of resolution' of problems by using the concept of strategy. Strategies can be defined as 'identifiable packages of action linked to broad, general aims' (Woods, 1980, p. 18); in other words, participants in classroom interaction solve everyday problems in ways which are consistent with their perspectives on the overall objectives of their activity. Over time, as these strategies enable participants to cope with the demands of interaction, they become embedded in actors' consciousness as ways of proceeding and ultimately become so routinized as to be totally taken for granted.

Teachers' Strategies

Several studies have suggested concrete examples of the strategies utilized by teachers in classrooms, although usually in the context of post-primary education. For example, Woods (1979) in a study of a secondary modern school, argues that teachers develop strategies to solve the problem of reconciling professional demands (for example, that teachers should educate pupils as individuals) with aspects of the social organization of schools and classrooms (for example, large classes, inadequate resources) which make the fulfilment of such demands difficult if not impossible. He documents eight strategies used by teachers in order to cope with the disjunction, such as 'domination', 'fraternization', 'occupational therapy' and even 'absence or removal'. Such strategies, Woods suggests, comprise a 'hidden pedagogy' which in a sense parallels the 'hidden curriculum' mentioned earlier, and whose purpose may be minimally concerned with official or professional goals. Rather, it may be intended to ensure sheer 'survival', although self-perceptions of commitment to, and a retrospective rhetoric of 'education' is maintained.

While in some cases strategies may be used for such purposes, even in less extreme circumstances participants in classrooms adopt strategies as ways of making classroom life as bearable and even rewarding as possible. Thus while not all the strategies of teachers suggested by Woods have been documented in primary schools, some certainly have, of which the use of dominative strategies is an obvious and common example. King's (1978) study of three infant schools provides evidence of three different types, of which physical domination was the least important but by no means unheard of:

> The smacking incident happened very quickly. Mrs Pink moved swiftly and surely to the mat where the boys were playing, and smacked Brian on the head. He is near to tears. (p. 54)

While such a physical approach may thus remain important in primary schools more common is the non-verbal technique of continuous scanning, by which teachers monitored the children's activities; as one said:

> Well you just can't afford to take your eyes off them, can you? There's no telling what they will be up to. You have to let them know you know what they are doing. (p. 51)

Thus often words were unnecessary to control:

The boy knocks over a jar of pencils on to the floor. He looks at the teacher. She looks at him. He picks up the pencils. (p. 50)

But the most common strategy of all for the domination of pupils is a verbal one. Teachers talk a lot, in some cases up to seventy or even eighty per cent of the time (Delamont, 1983, p. 115ff); one function of such talk is to impose the teacher's definition of the situation on to the classroom and to allow little opportunity for alternative pupil definitions (literally) to make themselves heard. King noted several types of such verbal control, often oblique in style, but nevertheless efficient. For example:

Make-a-game-of-it control: 'Boys close eyes. Girls creep out, quietly get your coats. Don't let the boys hear you!'

Joking control: 'Don't put your finger in there Mark (the chair strut), it will get fixed and we'll have to bring your tea here to you'.

Shaming control: A boy sucks his thumb. Teacher: 'Darren isn't singing today. He has a chocolate thumb.' Some children laugh. Darren does not.

Reference control: 'Put the apron on. What would Mummy say if you come home with paint on that nice new jumper?' (p. 52–3)

Such physical, non-verbal and verbal control strategies are all ways in which the teacher maintains domination of the children; in contrast Mrs White was unable to find effective strategies enabling her to impose her definition of the situation on the children. To the other teachers, events in her classroom provided evidence that effective control was essential if order was to be maintained. In Mrs White's classroom it was the pupils who were in control; she left teaching the next year.

Pupils' Strategies

The obverse of teacher strategies are those of pupils. Pupils too face problems of coming to terms with classroom interaction; as suggested earlier, the culture of the home or the peer group or both may not be ones which enable pupils to adapt easily or unequivocally to the classroom and the teacher. However, pupils are not usually in the position of developing strategies in order to fulfil relatively long-term goals, as teachers are. Rather, as Denscombe (1980) has argued, pupil strategies are adopted *in response to* those of teachers; they take the form of counter-strategies through which teachers' strategies can be negated or negotiated in order to construct a preferable classroom life. Woods (1977a) has suggested that pupils adopt one of five 'modes' or general orientations to classroom processes: conformity, retreatism, colonization, intransigency and rebellion, but once again these have been developed mainly in the context of secondary schools. In primary schools pupil strategies of noise, subversive or diversionary humour, negotiation and so on often occur within the framework of acceptance of and cooperation with the teacher. Delamont's (1983) comment that: 'the pupil's first strategy is to find out what the teacher wants and to give it to her' (p. 122) applies to many primary school classrooms. Perhaps the major motive for giving the teacher what she wants, in primary classrooms, is the desire for approval and praise. To achieve this, pupils work hard at discovering from the teacher's words and also from her gestures, facial expressions, etc., what responses will be regarded as acceptable. Even the very youngest pupils learn fast to assess what kind of answer or behaviour will satisfy the teacher and then proceed to provide it. The strategy pupils use is to assume that clues to acceptable words or actions are implicit in the organization of the classroom situation that they face; pupils thus operate by attempting to tune in to the teacher's definition of the situation in order to construct answers that will gain approval. In this extract from a tape-recording made by King (1978, pp 45–6) teacher and pupils are discussing a picture of a christening:

Teacher: Some people that are special people that have to go to a christening. Can anybody tell me what they are called? Special people that have to go to a . . . Karina?
Karina: Cousins.
Teacher: Yes, well, cousins would go but you have special people at your christening.
Pupil: Nannies.
Teacher: Nannies, come, yes!
Pupil: Parents.
Teacher: Yes, parents come but someone else very special.
Pupil: Cousins.
Teacher: Yes, we said cousins, Martin.
Pupil: The christening man.
Teacher: Oh yes, children!
Pupil: And christening man.

> *Teacher:* What do you call the christening man?
> *Pupil:* A vicar.
> *Teacher:* A vicar. That's right! That's the christening man
>   . . .

(Later in the transcript)

> *Joanna:* I've been to a christening with my auntie but it
>   wasn't their house, it was another house and we had lovely
>   teas.
> *Teacher:* Lovely teas, yes. Now Karina?
> *Karina:* When you sometimes you got to a christening you
>   can see which is a boy and a girl cause a girl has a long dress
>   and um a boy has a short dress.
> *Teacher:* Either a short dress or a little short suit. What
>   colour do we say for a boy as a rule?
> *Pupil:* White.
> *Pupil:* Blue.
> *Teacher:* Blue for a boy and what for a girl?
> *Pupil:* White
> *Pupil:* Green! Green!
> *Teacher:* White or?
> *Pupil:* Pink.
> *Teacher:* Pink! Pink! That's right.

There are a number of interesting implications even in such a short extract: the verbal dominance of the teacher by means of the preponderant use of questions to which only one answer is acceptable, often a technical term ('vicar'), and the concomitant rarity of questions enabling pupils to explore a range of different possibilities (indeed, contributions that lead away from the teacher's specific purpose are not pursued — 'Lovely teas, yes. Now Karina?'); approval and praise for correct responses often signalled by repetition ('A vicar. That's right!'); and even the reinforcing of sexual stereotypes ('Blue for a boy'). But most relevant here is the evidence of pupils' determination to use whatever cues are available (in a transcript necessarily only verbal ones appear, such as 'someone *else* very special', but in the actual situation others would also be available) to find the answer that will elicit approval from the teacher.

Strategies in the Classroom

The use and interrelationship of teachers' and pupils' strategies in classrooms is often rather more complex than appears from these relatively straightforward examples. In two articles Pollard has attempted to analyze more complicated issues. In the first (1979) he begins by pointing to the limitations of a view of interaction in the classroom as characterized by teacher domination and pupil subordination. Coercive strategies are certainly used by teachers, but also of significance is the way in which teachers and pupils whose interests differ (for example, teachers' need to maintain control, pupils' desire to avoid tedium) may nevertheless negotiate a 'working consensus', a 'collective interdependent adaption by the children and the teacher to the threat which they each pose to the other' (p. 78), which enables both to achieve acceptable resolutions and satisfactory compromises. The rules which govern the working consensus are not static but vary according to the 'mood' of the teacher, the curricular task in progress, the temporal phase of the activity, and the physical and material setting within which the interaction occurs.

Pollard goes on to suggest that deviance in primary school classrooms can be of two kinds: the first he calls routine deviance, i.e. actions which are censured as being inappropriate but which are within the boundaries of the working consensus:

Teacher: You can never get kids to be good all the time, it wouldn't be natural anyway.
Child: If we did just what we're meant to we'd get bored stiff, most of the teachers will have a bit of a laugh with us.
(p. 82)

Routine deviance, then, incorporates such pupil activities as talking, eating, jostling, fidgeting, failing to complete work, etc. Most pupils acknowledge these as constituting misbehaviour, and accept the legitimacy of teachers' routine censures. But sometimes actions by teachers or pupils may break the boundaries of this routine deviance and censure: the teacher may 'go mad', the pupils may 'act daft'. For example:

Child: If we get done it's not fair because the smelly gits never listen to what we have to say, they just play bloody hell. So we don't bother with 'em now, we just get on and mess about as much as we can (p. 83)

Thus the argument is that within the boundaries of the working consensus, pupils may conform to teachers' expectations and demands or may engage in routine deviance which teachers routinely censure; but either teachers or pupils may also unilaterally break the consensus. Pollard goes on to suggest that while most pupils rejected unilateral teacher action (such as humiliating pupils or being angrily sarcastic), they differed in the degree to which they were willing to enter into the working consensus. He views pupils as falling into one of three types: good groups, joker groups, and gangs. Good groups accepted the legitimacy of teachers' routine and sometimes even unilateral censures, whereas members of gangs rejected the latter and often the former too. The majority of children, however, took no hard and fast line of approval or disapproval of teachers' actions, but assessed their legitimacy in the context of use:

> *Child:* Well it all depends on what's been happening. . .
> *Child:* Sometimes it's fair and sometimes it isn't. . . (p. 88)

Such pupils, then, accept teachers' authority and censures within the boundaries of the negotiated consensus and their actions also rarely break such limits. Their strategies are designed to allow the possibility of achieving goals such as having a laugh, avoiding boredom, and maintaining individuality and a degree of autonomy without incurring serious penalties.

In his second paper (1980) Pollard focusses on how teachers approach and engage in the working consensus. He suggests that teacher interests (such as maintaining order so as to impress significant others, maintaining self-images as an educator in the face of practical realities militating against the achievement of educational goals, and conserving energy and avoiding stress or, more positively, enjoying classroom work) require the construction by the teacher of classroom routines, procedures and ways of doing things, since such routines are means by which his interests can be furthered. But routines constrain teachers as well as pupils; the teacher cannot step outside their boundaries without running the risk of losing the legitimacy usually accorded to him by pupils. The strategies embedded in the routines of the working consensus may not always enable the teacher to achieve his objectives of order, instruction and enjoyment: for example, having a laugh with pupils may be enjoyable for the teacher but may contribute to disorder; work routines may maintain order but not achieve educational objectives. For such reasons, Pollard argues, teachers attempt a balance of interests by 'juggling' priorities, thus maximizing the satisfaction that can be achieved within a specific context of interaction. He provides an example of such juggling from a lesson in which the children were asked to write a story. Initially the teacher is friendly, joking with the children and motivating them to satisfy his requirements in the task. However, as the lesson proceeds, it becomes clear that many of the children are making mistakes in punctuation. The mood changes to one of crisis; the teacher's instructional interests are not being achieved and he explodes in anger at one child; 'the act of getting angry serves the teacher's self-interests primarily by giving vent to frustration and also by replacing the stress and confusion of the crisis with a clear assertion to his power' (p. 57). But the teacher follows this up by returning to the strategy of appeal used at the beginning of the lesson; his 'overall judgment in this crisis was to cut his instructional losses for the lesson, to reassert the 'appeal' tone in the hope of getting more from its strategies in the other lessons of the day' (p. 56).

Language in the Classroom

At this point something more specific needs to be said about language in the primary classroom, although it has been an implicit theme in much of this chapter. While the analysis of language comprises very complex issues (see Stubbs, 1983 for a fuller discussion) and while sociolinguistic work has been attempted in education, for some reason, mainly with either pre-school or secondary school children, several persistent themes in such work can be identified and illustrated in the context of primary classrooms. The first and obvious point is that language is central to what goes on in classrooms. As suggested earlier, teachers in particular talk for a great deal of the time, and it is indeed very difficult to imagine a teacher in the classroom who did not talk at all. But more specifically, the language used by teachers is typically rather different from that found in other social settings. Take, for example, an exchange recorded in an infant school:

Teacher: Children. What did I say? Children. What did I say yesterday about all shouting out together? Can I listen (*raising her voice*) to everybody talking at once?
Pupils: (*in chorus*) No.
Teacher: How many people can I listen to at once?
Pupils: (*breaking in before she finished*) One.
Teacher: One. And what happens if everybody shouts at once?

Pupils: Can't hear.
Teacher: I can't hear *anybody*. (Willes, 1981, p. 56)

This encounter, routine for a classroom of young children, would sound very odd in another social situation; think for example of the host of a dinner party addressing his guests in such terms. A central characteristic of teachers' talk then is that they ask questions to which they already know the answers. The same kind of approach can be seen very clearly in the transcript from King's study examined earlier. The following exchange is worth another look:

Teacher: What do you call the christening man?
Pupil: A vicar
Teacher: A vicar. That's right. That's the christening man...

Here not only does the teacher ask a question to which she already knows the answer but does so using a very common format; initiation, response, feedback, or IRF for short. Such exchanges are ubiquitous in classrooms. It can also be seen that the teacher is asking a *closed* question — there is only one right answer that she will accept. It is much less easy to find examples of *open* teacher questions to which there are a variety of possible acceptable answers, or teacher questions which are exploratory or tentative. There are, of course, good reasons for both the IRF pattern and for the preponderance of closed questions: many teachers regard their job as that of initiating pupils into bodies of knowledge to which the teacher (alone) has access. Such approaches thus make it easier for teachers to achieve and maintain control both in terms of knowledge and in terms of discipline.

Classroom language of these kinds is relatively easy to record and analyze, but it has been suggested that much of the talk in classrooms (especially in less formal lessons) is confused, fragmented and ambiguous. One reason for this is that participants in classrooms are immersed in a social context in which language is only one of several ways of conveying meaning (gestures, looks, and posture are all significant too). It can, therefore, be argued that the meaning of speech cannot be read off unambiguously from transcripts, but is embedded in the totality of the situation. One interesting attempt to overcome such limitations is by using visual records (i.e. film) of classroom interaction. These, alongside transcripts or audio recordings, provide a much more sophisticated account, especially of pupils' language which is shown to be both complex and varied (see for example Walker and Adelman, 1975). Such work still demonstrated, however, that teachers' voices tend to dominate even when they are trying not to be intrusive, as can be seen by comparing children's discussion with and without the presence of a teacher (for example, Ede and Williamson, 1980, pp. 220–33; see also Willes, 1983).

Conclusion

As suggested at the beginning of this chapter, it is clear that much sociological work remains to be accomplished on teachers, pupils and their interaction in classrooms. Much of the research, particularly that concerning pupils and also that concerning the actions of teachers *outside* the classroom, is rather fragmentary, and indicative of problems yet to be fully worked out rather than being conclusive. Nevertheless, many of these studies demonstrate the complexity of what may appear at first glance to be a straightforward task of making sense of the everyday routines and practices of classrooms. Further, in contrast to the research considered in chapter 4, they hint at the range, subtlety and variety of action and interaction in schools, action which cannot sensibly be summarized by labels like 'group instructor' or 'formal teacher', however methodologically pure such categories may be. Teachers and pupils, like other human beings, are active creators of meaning not passive objects to be appropriately fitted into one or other type or box. As meaning creators, people in schools have hopes and fears, ideas and beliefs, emotions and ambitions, all of which are highly relevant to what happens in the classroom. In other words, the processual nature of life in classrooms, the fact that all actions have a history and a biography, an intention and a meaning is at least acknowledged.

However, one germane criticism of ethnographic and interactionist studies of the kind discussed in this chapter is that they may view the classroom as an island insulated from external events and forces, and not as intricately bound up with social processes in general. The question of the implications and effects of primary schooling, and its overall relationship to the wider society needs to be addressed more directly; these issues are considered in chapter 6.

Summary

A range of sociological studies of classroom life has been published in recent years, studies which although varying in many respects, indicate how complicated and subtle the processes of classroom interaction are. For example, one important theme of research on teachers has been the attempt to explain the apparent irrationality of teachers' action, the fact that teachers operate on the basis of intuition rather than careful intellectual analysis. It has been argued that such approaches by teachers are necessary, in the sense that only thus can teachers deal with the day to day pressures of classroom events; or alternatively that such methods are means by which teachers cope with the inherent uncertainty of their professional work. While such explanations are plausible, it has also been convincingly argued that researchers have misunderstood teachers' action: teachers in fact act logically and rationally but in terms of a different, context-bound logic which requires subtle investigation to uncover and explicate. Similarly, while little research on pupils has been completed, an essential theme of recent studies of children's culture is the underlying seriousness and rationality of what are apparently confused and inchoate events.

The concept of strategy has been used in a number of studies of classroom interaction; one of its virtues is that it focusses attention on the ways in which participants in classrooms rationally pursue aims, make sense of events, and engage in activities, rather than the researcher erecting some reified concept of logical action which teachers and pupils do not attain. Pollard's work, for example, makes very clear that teachers and pupils make sense of their own and each other's action in terms of a complex pattern of interaction, the working consensus. In contrast, then, to research considered earlier, such studies contribute to a fuller sociological understanding of classroom life; it remains, however, to discuss the relationship of such processes to the social structure in general.

6   The Effects of Primary Education

A central debate of the sociology of education in the last thirty or more years has related to questions of the differential achievement of pupils of various social class (and recently ethnic and gender) groups in and beyond education. The fact that children from working class backgrounds generally achieve less through education in terms of the achievement of academic credentials in school, entry to and success in higher education and high status occupations than do children from middle class homes is not a matter of dispute (see for example, Tyler, 1977 and Rubinstein, 1979). However, analyses of such educational and social inequality have proposed a huge range of possible causes and an equally diverse array of remedies. For example, it has been suggested that central to the relative failure of working class children in schools is inadequate early socialization in the home; forms of language development inappropriate for educational purposes; the inferior genetic intellectual inheritance characteristic of children from certain racial and/or social groups; unsupportive parental attitudes towards school; organizational practices within schools, notably streaming; and even the structure of capitalist societies and endemic class conflict. While some writers have argued that educational inequality is functionally necessary for the maintenance or even survival of society, more commonly proposals have been made to remedy such inequality. Once again, they are very diverse: for example, it has been argued that intervention in the child's first few years of life is necessary in order to'compensate' for the inadequacies of the home; that the tripartite system of secondary education should be replaced by comprehensive schools, *or* that such replacement has destroyed working class children's best hope of academic achievement; that education should be totally de-institutionalized and compulsory schools should be replaced by voluntary learning networks; that the revolutionary transformation of western capitalist economies is a necessary precondition of meaningful educational reform.

The complexities of the debate surrounding these issues have been usefully discussed by Tyler (1977); as in other areas of educational discussion the focus of interest has not usually been in the context of primary education, but nevertheless some very diverse approaches have been utilized. For Parsons (1959) the function of the elementary school is to differentiate pupils in terms of their achievement at intellectual tasks and in terms of their success at adopting the values of the adult society as represented by the teacher; the achieving child is both 'bright' and behaves responsibly: the good pupils 'is defined in terms of a fusion of the cognitive and the moral components' (p. 440). Such differentiation, which is built upon by the secondary school, is neither a sociological nor a moral problem:

> it is fair to give differential rewards for different levels of achievement, so long as there has been fair access to opportunity, and fair that these rewards lead on to higher-order opportunities for the successful ... the elementary school class is an embodiment of the fundamental American value of equality of opportunity (p. 445)

More recent sociological writers have denied each of Parsons' assertions: centrally, the notion that schools embody equality of opportunity has been challenged.

Teachers' Expectations

One argument that has recently been popular, for example, is that the differentiation of pupils reflects not so much unproblematic cognitive and moral achievement as the conscious or unconscious predisposition of teachers to favour children who are most like themselves (i.e. usually middle class rather than working class). Thus, it has been suggested, teachers tend to use different classroom strategies with pupils from different social classes with consequently varying effects; there is some research which suggests that in the long term such different strategies function to separate out groups of pupils on the basis of social class. Essentially, then, the argument is that teachers' *expectations* influence the behaviour of pupils — and thus that such expectations in themselves have the consequence that favoured groups of children make greater academic progress. Examples of work which addresses this theme are the studies by Rist

(1970) in the USA, Goodacre (1968) in England and Nash (1973) in Scotland.

Rist's research focussed on what happened to a group of black children in their first two and a half years in school in a 'blighted urban area'. On the children's eighth day they were arranged by the teacher in permanent groups seated at tables. Table One consisted of those children that the teacher thought of as 'fast learners', whereas some of Table Two and all of Table Three were those pupils that she felt 'had no idea of what was going on in the classroom' (p. 422). Such teacher decisions were not based on any test or formal assessment but on quite informal criteria none of which related directly to the individual children's intellectual ability or attainment. Thus, those children who interacted with adults easily, those who spoke Standard American English, those who were neat and clean (and did not smell) and those who had parents who were educated, employed, living together and interested in the child's education, tended to be allocated to Table One. Those children deficient in such characteristics, and thus further from the teacher's 'ideal type' of the successful pupil, ended up on Table Two or Three. Now in practice the teacher concentrated her pedagogical attention on Table One children, whereas Tables Two and Three children received more control utterances — on one occasion an hour went by in the classroom in which no child at Table Two or Three was spoken to by the teacher at all, except to be told to sit down. The children at Table One began to belittle and ridicule the others, while the children at Tables Two and Three became more physically and verbally hostile and tended to withdraw from interaction with the teacher even when she initiated it. Not all the children progressed to the next class in their second year in school but when those who did were divided into Tables (A, B and C this time) no child who had been on Table Two or Three was 'promoted' to Table A. Again, not all the children moved up a class at the end of the second year, but those who did were divided into groups with names: the top group was called the Tigers, the second group the Cardinals and, believe it or not, the third group the Clowns. Again none of the Table B or C children moved up to join the Tigers. So on the basis of streaming practices by one teacher after eight days in school, children's future academic attainment was crucially affected. Some children proceeded from Table One to Table A to the Tigers, and received the benefits of disproportionate teacher time and effort. Other less favoured children were provided with a rather inferior educational experience on the basis of selection after eight days schooling.

It may be that in British primary schools processes of teacher expectation are more subtle but several studies suggest that they exist. Goodacre (1968) for example, in a study of the teaching of reading in infants' schools, compared teachers' evaluations of children's reading attainment with their actual reading attainment as measured on various reading tests. She found that many children from working class backgrounds could read better than their teachers gave them credit for. Teachers' assessments of and expectations for pupils' reading ability were influence by their informal estimates of home circumstances, father's occupation, parental interest, and so on (estimates which were not based on experience since very few of the teachers had ever visited the children's homes). The teachers were thus estimating and assessing children's reading on the basis of expectations partly based on what they had picked up about the children's home background. As a result they were underestimating the capabilities of at least some children from working class homes.

In Nash's (1973) research, not only did children who the teacher believed came from 'poor' homes do worse academically than those they though came from 'good' homes, but he also provides some evidence as to the mechanisms by which this process operated, showing how children were treated characteristically differently within the classroom, as in the cases of Robert and Jamie:

Observation record 3 Robert
Most of the class are doing project work. Three boys still seen to be doing English. This means they haven't finished quickly enough. Teacher looks over to them. 'Robert, you could be doing an excellent drawing for me but you're so slow with your English.' Robert looks glum. He puts down his pencil. Looks like he's finished at last — or given up. He goes to the teacher who is telling Albert what a 'lovely wee campfire' he has painted. She sees Robert standing a bit behind her not drawing attention to himself. 'Ah, now you can help me here, she says. She heads him over to the model tray. We're going to have Rockies either side and that's going to be a wee pass. Are you very good at making mountain shapes?' Robert looks doubtfully at the heap of papier mache. 'No? asks the teacher. 'Well, I'll get someone else to do that then.' She tells him to do a picture instead. Robert goes back to his desk. He looks about, sees that he hasn't any paper to draw on and decides to finish his English. A couple of minutes later teacher

asks the class, 'Anyone still doing English?' Robert raises his hand. 'Oh come on, Robert,' she says. (p. 33)

Nash comments that much of Robert's time in school resembles this ten minute period. Clearly Robert is unhappy and unsuccessful in school, but this is partly due to the way the teacher organizes the classroom — he is kept writing while others are doing art and craft; when he tries to get something of more interest to do the teacher offers him something and then immediately withdraws the offer, presumably because she thinks he can't cope with it. The she gives him work to do which he cannot manage because of lack of materials, and then she gets cross because he appears slow. Thus the teacher's unfavourable perceptions of Robert lead her to set up expectations for him which are fulfilled in part *because* of the perceptions themselves. In contrast, Jamie fares better:

Observation record 4 Jamie
Jamie is at the teacher's desk. He talks to Ian who has just got up. They compare their work. John, in front of Jamie, joins in. They talk energetically but in lowered voices. Jamie watches the teacher closely as she marks John's book. He refers to his book and makes several alterations, corrections I expect, with his pencil. Teacher takes his book. 'Right', she says. Then, 'Some of you are not using very sharp pencils. I can hardly read it'. Quickly she corrects his work. 'Jamie, there you are'. Jamie takes his book and goes over to the box to replace his workcard. He returns to his desk. He flicks through his record book at ticks off the answers. One of the boys in the quene asks him a question and Jamie pauses to answer and talks to him for a few moments. The teacher asks who is talking. 'I just can't concentrate with this noise whoever it is,' she says. Jamie contines with his work. The class quieten down. There are about twenty people now around the teacher's desk. The noise grows louder again. The teacher warns the class adding, 'Shirley I don't want that shrieking.' Jamie works quietly for three or four minutes until the teacher has marked most of the books. She gives up half-way through and tells everyone to sit down. The class are now given instructions about the project they are to do. Everybody is going to write diaries of a Western pioneer family. 'I'm going to put you in families. Husbands and wives — there's no need to be silly about it — and children.' She looks round to see who has finished the English work.

'Right,' she says, 'Jamie, you pick your waggon.' Jamie grins and stands up and makes great play over picking his friends who move over to his desk. (pp. 34–5)

In this rather different case Nash comments that because Jamie is quick with his work and because of the way that the classroom is structured, he has only a little time to wait in the queue enabling him to complete his record book for which he will later be rewarded. When Jamie's talking disturbs the teacher she comments to the whole class but does not mention his name — she says: 'I just can't concentrate with this noise *whoever it is*'. But when a less favoured child disturbs her she is warned by name: 'Shirley, I don't want that shrieking'. Shirley is thus reprimanded, Jamie is not. He than gets first choice in choosing a family which in the eyes of the children is a substantial reward. Nash concludes that he is not implying conscious discrimination or bias on the part of the teacher. The activities and processes of her classroom are, however, the result of her beliefs that Jamie is very able and that Robert is not. Inevitably her actions are affected by such beliefs.

While the evidence provided by writers like Goodacre and Nash is hardly conclusive, and some of it has indeed been specifically questioned on the basis of the 'ORACLE' data (Croll, 1981), it does suggest that teachers' expectations may be powerful. If, for whatever reason, teachers assume that polite and well-dressed middle class children are more likely to be educationally successful than less deferential or less tidy pupils, then this asumption in itself may affect teachers' behaviour towards those children in the classroom. Such differential treatment over long periods of time may affect pupils' academic attainment. In such ways, then, teachers may quite unconsciously enhance the academic performance of those who they expect to do well and simultaneously depress the standards of work they obtain from those for whom they are not so optimistic.

There have been two kinds of reaction to evidence of this kind. The first one might call the 'teacher-bashing' response. This suggests that teachers allow their prejudices to operate in a most reprehensible way; what they should do is, like Boxer in George Orwell's *Animal Farm*, to try harder not to do such nasty things to children. The second and perhaps more adequate response is that it is in fact *impossible* for teachers faced with large numbers of children to efficiently manage, control and teach them all as individuals, so they use whatever cues (social class, sex) are available as ways of sorting children into manageable groups. In other words, the real reason why some children are more favourably treated than others is because there simply isn't enough time and energy to devote to all the children equally. Some other (mainly Marxist) accounts develop these themes within the framework of a rather more sophisticated theory of primary schooling.

Marxist Approaches

It has been suggested by writers within the Marxist tradition (for example, Bowles and Gintis, 1976) that schools are a central means by which the socio-economic order characteristic of capitalist societies is reproduced. Thus, for example, traditional schooling is a system which ensures that most children fail through practices such as streaming, highly competitive examinations, highly abstract and academic curricula, the 11+ examination and so on. This reflects the demands of the economy for a small elite of highly educated and socialized people for positions of power and privilege and for a larger mass of workers to fill monotonous and ill-paid jobs. But the function of the traditional school is not only to differentiate between such an elite and the rest in order to reproduce the economic order, but also to make it appear that such differentiation is entirely right, proper and just. Schools say to children, in effect, if you fail in school it is because of your own inadequacies, your own stupidity, rather than as is in fact the case an entirely inevitable consequence of the particular structure of educational arrangements that exist within capitalist societies. While Bowles and Gintis's account has been much criticized (not least by Marxists) Sharp and Green's (1975) argument derives from within the broad framework of assumptions of such an analysis. They suggest that the practice of progressive infant education, far from contributing to a more open class structure in which each individual is valued for his own qualities and attainments, actually results in kinds of hierarchical differentiation very similar to those characteristic of traditional teacher-pupil relationships.

As stated earlier, Sharp and Green's study was based on participant observation and interviews in a progressive London primary school. Most of the authors' attention is focussed on three infants' classes, although they also present material based on interviews with the headteacher and with parents. The constraints of the classroom situation (notably the sheer number of children in each class) made it impossible for the teacher to treat and respond to every child individually, and so those who fitted the teachers' concept of 'normality' tended to be differentiated from those who in teachers' language were 'thick' or 'peculiar'. The child's motivation, appearance and behaviour in school reinforced such stereotypes; teachers regarded as 'normal' children who were easily controlled and who could anticipate the teacher's requirements. The 'thick' ones were those who were not motivated by the activities the teacher defined as important. Since it was the 'normal' children with whom the teachers felt both at ease and successful, they were favoured in terms of teacher attention within the classroom. On the other hand the 'problem' children tended to be left alone until such time as they were 'ready'. Since such children received less attention they had little opportunity to acquire different and more favourable teacher categorization and thus their deviant identities tended to stick. In practice, the view that some children could only 'work through' their problems alone reinforced their isolation within the classroom. Thus the paradox was that while the teachers' rhetoric stressed the value and significance of the individual child, their practice stratified children, selecting out certain individuals and 'cooling out' others. For example, an interesting contrast is provided by examining teachers' accounts of first a favoured and then an unfavoured child. Sylvia is one of the children:

> who likes to spend rather a lot of time with me, you know; if they could, they would be with me all the time and always doing the activities (by this she is referring to the activities she sets up, small projects of art and craft work, etc.). The sort of children you like to have doing things with you because they want to. (p. 143)

In contrast, Glen was a problem:

> He wouldn't attempt anything. He just didn't seem to be interested in anything. He wouldn't speak to anybody. He does anything under sufferance. He won't draw much because he's not very good, he rarely paints a picture, or plays with the Lego, he just wanders around ... He doesn't talk much to me. I don't think he likes me very much. If you try to talk to him he just looks straight through you. (pp. 155–6)

Thus the actual practice of teaching within classrooms (concentration on children regarded as receptive, the abandonment of 'problem' children to their own devices with consequent persistence of deviance and differential attainment reinforcing the original stereotype) resulted in the hierarchical differentiation of pupils: 'whilst the teacher displays a moral concern that every child matters, in practice there is a subtle process of sponsorship developing where opportunity is being offered to some and closed off to others. Social stratification is emerging' (p. 218). The ideology of progressivism adopted by the teachers is viewed by Sharp and Green as a 'romantic radical conservatism' which legitimates new ways of achieving old goals, new ways of legitimating inequality in a society in which ascribed inequality is no longer easy to justify but inequality on apparent merit is acceptable. However, Sharp and Green do not view such practices essentially as arising from the idiosyncrasies of misguided teachers, but from structural factors — within the school the need for management and control and the fact of large classes which makes individualized contact with all the pupils difficult if not impossible, and in a wider context the 'social demands of established interests in the macro-structure' (p. 224).

Sharp and Green's work is important because of its attempt to relate aspects of primary education to more general social theory; it has, however, been substantially criticized. Hargreaves (1978) for example, has argued that the kinds of abstract and decontextualized questions typically asked of teachers by Sharp and Green themselves produce the confusion and 'inadequacy' of answer which is then used as evidence of a disjunction between teachers' rhetoric and their practice. Further, he argues that even if it is accepted that teachers are subject to a variety of constraints and limitations on their actions, constraints which lead to practices which in effect stratify pupils, there are no convincing reasons or evidence to assume that these directly reflect 'social demands of established interests'. Who or what these interests represent, and how their demands are articulated in classrooms is very unclear.

A rather similar argument to that of Sharp and Green is developed by Kanter (1972) in a study of children from professional families in an American nursery school run on the basis of neo-Freudian ideas of eliminating experiences which would hinder children's fragile developing emotional maturity. The result of such a system was that the children were immersed in experiences resembling those characteristic of large-scale bureaucratic organizations. The stress on routine, the attempts to limit uncertainty, strangeness and personal accountability all functioned to accustom the children to the structural conditions of adult society. The nursery school, then, implemented theories which fitted with patterns of organization of the wider society, and functioned to prepare children for that society.

However, King (1978) has argued that accounts of these kinds, whether functionalist or Marxist, which view the long term effects of education as explaining classroom processes, are inadequate because neither encompasses the complexity of human interaction in the classroom: there is 'little to choose between being the "cultural dope" of functionalism or suffering from the "false consciousness" of Marxism' (p. 130). King's own study is grounded in the social theory of Weber. His conclusion is that the education of infant school aged children has in terms of personal relationships, expectations of behaviour and work, and so on, a greater affinity to typical practice in middle rather than working class homes. Such a conclusion, while more cautious and modest than that of Sharp and Green, nevertheless appears to complement their work.

Class and Pedagogy

The most complex and ambitious attempt to conceptualize the relationship between aspects of primary education and society is that of Bernstein's (1975) paper 'Class and pedagogies: visible and invisible'. He begins by characterizing the 'invisible' pedagogy of infants' classrooms as one in which teacher control is implicit rather than explicit, where the teacher arranges a context of learning within which the child organizes his own work, movement and social relationships, where the transmission of specific skills is not much emphasized, and where criteria of evaluation of pedagogical achievement are diffuse and multiple. Essentially, *overt* teacher control, transmission of knowledge, criteria of evaluation, and so on are replaced by forms of control, etc., which are implicit and covert. The rules of the classroom game are much less obvious to children (or parents) but have to be inferred and intuited: smashing up the classroom furniture is still disapproved of. Central to the invisible pedagogy is children's play. *How* the child plays, his individual response to the classroom contexts, is utilized as a crucial criterion of his performance and achievement. The teacher, then, is engaged in a constant surveillance of the child, the results of which are interpreted as demonstrating the degree of 'readiness' (i.e. developmental stage) the child has attained. The invisible pedagogy is thus a pervasive one: more of the pupil's characteristics and personality are legitimate aspects of teacher control and less can be regarded as private and not of concern to the school and the teacher. Bernstein argues that play is not sharply distinguished from work, and one implication may be that children from working class homes where play and work are typically rigidly distinguished may be at a disadvantage in an apparently fluid and open classroom situation, vis a vis middle class children. Working class parents too are less likely to understand the principles on which the invisible pedagogy is based and in turn may be regarded by teachers as irrelevant or harmful to their children's education.

Bernstein's major purpose is to explain the invisible pedagogy as arising from the interests of what he calls the 'new' middle class, distinguished from the old property and capital owning middle class by being involved in service occupations, especially those which control communication (presumably such areas as the media and education itself, although this is not clear). He argues in a commentary on his own paper that:

> That fraction of the middle class which has gained access to the area of symbolic control (specialized and dominant forms of communication) selects from prevailing forms of the socialization of the young those forms which encourage children to display their diversity and to learn the subtleties and strategies of inter- and intra-personal control. Such forms of socialization are legitimized by a group of theories thought to be progressive within the spectrum of the social sciences. From one point of view this is the origin of the 'spontaneous' child apparently putting it together in his own way. From another point of view, such a form of socialization enables parents to screen the child's possibilities so that they, and the child later, can take advantage of the diversification of the occupational structure of symbolic control (p. 19).

The conflict between new and old middle classes, arising from their different relations to economic production, is a struggle not over the *relationship* of classes but of the *forms* of their intergenerational reproduction. As adults within the new middle class are in an anomalous class position, they require a socialization for their children which is varied, expressive and flexible, which in turn will enable them to find a way to a high position within the class structure.

This paper by Bernstein is one of a series in which he is grappling with issues concerning the transmission of culture in the context of education. Such issues are of a complexity that the difficult and abstract nature of his writing is understandable, even though it is hard to judge whether this particular article is, as some have suggested, brilliant but rather confused or as others have alleged simply obscure. King (1979) in particular has argued that his own empirical research, referred to earlier, provides little support for Bernstein's theoretical generalizations. Specifically, the latter's assertions that the pedagogy of teachers in infants' classrooms involves a diminution in the teaching of particular skills, a high degree of child control over work, movement and relationships, and that play and work are sharply distinguished, are all incorrect as descriptions of practice in the schools studied by King (and all have also been contradicted by research discussed in chapter 4 of this book). Bernstein's apparent misunderstanding of actual practice in classrooms, as different from what teachers say or imply is the ideological basis of their work ('the theology of the infant school') is a consequence of theoretical work which is not directly informed by empirical research. Nevertheless, Bernstein's work represents, along with that of Sharp and Green, a valuable attempt to theorize primary education in a way that connects it with central sociological issues such as class, power and social control. It is a broad sweep of an analysis which can only be substantiated or modified or discarded on the basis of a vast amount of empirical work. Such research, as we have seen, is only just beginning.

Summary

Questions about the effects of schooling have been central to the sociology of education in Britain. Little consensus in the area exists, and a variety of causes of and remedies for the disjunction in educational achievement between children from working class and middle class homes have been suggested. One explanation, in terms of teachers' differential expectations of children from different social groups, has recently been popular, and other mainly Marxist writers have placed such an explanation within the context of structural rather than individual factors. The works of both Sharp and Green and Bernstein, although rather different in approach, valuably focus on the relationship between processes within classroom and broader social and economic changes. Both accounts have been substantially criticized, but they indicate nevertheless the value of attempts to understand and explain primary education and primary schools in terms of sociological theory.

7 Conclusion

In this book it has been argued that the structure, organization and processes of current primary education are related to the social conditions of the past and of the present. State-provided primary education emerged from idealist ideological assumptions, and has slowly changed and developed. In one sense the Plowden Report was a culmination of this process, in that it encapsulated progressive ideas and reflected the ideologies of a society much changed since the late nineteenth century. Subsequent social change, however, has led to an assertion of neo-idealist ideological accounts, which have become increasingly pervasive and which have led to further (but different) changes in schools and in the system as a whole. However, reports that primary education has at any time been transformed wholesale are clearly mistaken.

Further, it has been argued that studies of teaching and learning in primary schools utilizing the concept of teaching style are of limited value, particularly in that they do not contribute much to a sociological account of primary education. In contrast, some recent work using various concepts and methodologies but consistently attempting to take into account the perspectives of participants within *their* social world, is of great interest, although connections between processes within primary school classrooms and the wider social structure are not yet fully developed.

Thus, one of the major purposes of this book has been to suggest, in contrast to the view that primary schools are simple and straightforward institutions which almost anyone can make sense of, that the sheer complexity and diversity of primary schools has not so far been comprehended let alone fully analyzed. As Richards (1979) has argued, until recently a 'tyranny of over-simplification' has characterized public and professional discussion of primary education, preventing adequate debate about the subtle and complicated processes of primary schools. That Richards is right can be clearly seen in the whole debate surrounding Plowden and the belief in a progressive 'takeover'. In contrast to such superficial and misleading ideas it has been argued that some recent studies, although arising from within different theoretical paradigms, adopting various methodologies, and arriving at assorted conclusions nevertheless represent one fruitful course for future sociological analysis of primary education. Although there are large gaps in the empirical research, some of which have been pointed to in the course of this book, perhaps more seriously the analysis of aspects of primary schooling in terms of theories derived from sociological analyses of other sectors of education and the generation of theories specific to the experience of teachers and pupils in primary schools had hardly begun. An agenda for the future of the sociology of primary education might therefore include topics such as the construction of social order in classrooms, staffrooms and playgrounds; the curriculum of the primary school; the long term implications of primary schooling for participants, especially children; the mapping of power relationships within schools; and so on — the list could be extended almost indefinitely. The work discussed in this book, such as that of Sharp and Green (1975), Bernstein (1975) and the Berlaks (1981) represents tantalizing starting points for such analyses.

While implications for future sociological work can be derived from such work, there are also implications for the professional work of teachers in schools. It was suggested in the Introduction that one possible response to the increasing public visibility and accountability of primary schools was to close the classroom door and concentrate on the immediate and fulfilling work of educating young children. This is perhaps an inadequate response; while this is not the place for the advocacy of specific political strategies and tactics for teachers, the evidence of the history of primary education suggests that without informed professional action both locally and nationally the interests of primary schools and those who work within them may be neglected. As Razzell (1979) has suggested:

> The story of primary education over the past fifty years is one of neglect and of struggle for recognition. Most people have tended to regard the teaching of young children as a simple and unsophisticated activity. (p. 119)

Unless teachers can generate an informed understanding of primary education the view that primary school teaching is an easy and straightforward task will persist. Further, an increased understanding of the processes within and outside schools may be valuable in terms of increasing teachers' professional pedagogic competence: the work of, for example, Bronwyn Davies and the Berlaks may have important practical utility for teachers' work.

Finally, it is easy to forget that primary schooling as a separate stage of the education system has only been in existence for a relatively short time. Even so, schools have changed in that time and are currently changing. The future is uncertain but teachers both individually and collectively as well as sociologists have an important contribution to make to the changes likely in the next decades.

Further Reading

If the reader's interest has been whetted by this book a brief list of texts recommended for following up themes and issues relating to primary education may be less daunting than the full bibliography.

Novels are an often neglected source of insight into schools; there are a number written for children which provide acute (and often very funny) accounts of primary classrooms. For example, Bernard Ashley's *The Trouble with Donovan Croft* (Puffin, 1974), Andrew Davies' *Marmalade and Rufus* (Abelard, 1979) and Gene Kemp's *The Turbulent Term of Tyke Tiler* (Puffin, 1977) are highly recommended.

A straightforward and readable introduction to contemporary primary education in the UK, broadly sympathetic to the ideas of Plowden is:

Pluckrose, H. (1979) *Children in their Primary Schools*, Harmondsworth, Penguin.

Another introductory book, which usefully summarizes much educational research relating to primary education is:

Boydell, D. (1978) *The Primary Teacher in Action*, London, Open Books.

Three books which approach primary schooling from within the framework of educational disciplines other than sociology (respectively philosophy, psychology and curriculum studies) and each of which is accessible and illuminating although a little more technical than Pluckrose or Boydell are:

Blenkin, G.M. and Kelly, A.V. (1981) *The Primary Curriculum*, London, Harper and Row.
Dearden, R.F. (1968) *The Philosophy of Primary Education*,

London, Routledge and Kegan Paul.
Donaldson, M. (1978) *Children's Minds* Glasgow, Fontana.

Two very useful books, the first a collection of articles and the second an extended discussion, which look to the future of primary education and also engage with some of the issues raised in this book are:

Richards, C. (Ed) (1982) *New Directions in Primary Education*, Lewes, Falmer Press.
Alexander, R. (1984) *Primary Teaching*, Eastbourne, Holt, Rinehart and Winston.

Also forward looking, but in a rather different way, is a fascinating and intensive study of children's work in one classroom where the teacher utilized progressive styles. The book is not a sociological study, but it provides many sociological insights into classroom processes:

Armstrong, M. (1980) *Closely Observed Children*, London Writers and Readers Publishing Cooperative.

Three empirical studies are particularly well worth reading, both for the thought-provoking ways in which they contradict each other and for the equally interesting respects in which they are complementary:

Berlak, A. and H. (1981) *Dilemmas of Schooling: Teaching and Social Change*, London, Methuen.
King, R. (1978) *All Things Bright and Beautiful? A Sociological Study of Infants' Classrooms*, Chichester, John Wiley.
Sharp, R. and Green, A. (1975) *Education and Social Control: A Study of Progressive Primary Education*, London, Routledge and Kegan Paul.

Finally, there is an excellent journal devoted to primary education, which consistently carries very useful articles. *Education 3–13* is published twice a year by Studies in Education Ltd., Nafferton, Driffield, North Humberside.

Bibliography

ACKER, S. (1983) 'Women and teaching: a semi-detached sociology of a semi-profession', in WALKER, S. and BARTON, L. (Eds) *Gender Class and Education*, Lewes, Falmer Press.

AITKEN, M., BENNETT, N., and HESKETH, J. (1981) 'Teaching styles and pupil progress: a reanalysis,' *British Journal of Educational Psychology*, 51.

ALEXANDER, R., (1984) *Primary Teaching*, Eastbourne, Holt, Rinehart and Winston.

ALLEN, I. *et. al.* (1975) *Working an Integrated Day*, London, Ward Lock.

ARMSTRONG, M., (1980) *Closely Observed Children*, London, Writers and Readers.

ASHTON, P. *et. al.* (1975) *The Aims of Primary Education: A Study of Teachers' Opinions*, London, Macmillan.

ASHTON, P. (1978) 'What are primary teachers' aims?,' in RICHARDS, C. (Ed) *Education 3–13*, Driffield, Nafferton Books.

ASHTON, P. (1981) 'Primary teachers' aims 1969–77,' in SIMON, B. and WILLCOCKS, J. (Eds) *Research and Practice in the Primary Classroom*, London, Routledge and Kegan Paul.

AULD, R. (1976) *William Tyndale Junior and Infants Schools Public Inquiry: A Report to the Inner London Education Authority*, London, ILEA.

BARKER-LUNN, J. (1970) *Streaming in the Primary School*, Slough, NFER.

BARKER-LUNN, J. (1982) 'Junior schools and their organizational policies,' *Educational Research*, 24, 4.

BARTON L. AND WALKER, S. (1978) 'Sociology of education at the crossroads', *Educational Review*, 30, 3.

BASSETT, G. (1970) *Innovation in Primary Education*, London, Wiley.

BASSEY, M. (1978) *Nine Hundred Primary School Teachers*, Slough, NFER.

BEALING, D. (1972) 'The organization of Junior school classrooms', *Educational Research*, 14, 4.

BECKER, H. (1952) 'Social-class variations in the teacher-pupil relationship,' in COSIN B. *et. al.* (Eds) *School and Society*, London, Routledge and Kegan Paul/Open University Press, 1971.

BECKER, H. (1953) 'The teacher in the authority system of the public school,' in HAMMERSLEY, M. and WOODS, P. (Eds) *The Process of Schooling*, London, Routledge and Kegan Paul/Open University Press, 1976.

BENNETT, N. (1976) *Teaching Styles and Pupil Progress*, London, Open Books.

BENNETT, N. *et. al.* (1980) 'Open plan primary schools, findings and implications of a national inquiry,' *Education 3–13*, 8, 1.

BENNETT, N. and ENTWISTLE, N. (1977) 'Rite and wrong: a reply to "A chapter of errors",' *Educational Research*, 19, 3.

BENNETT, N. and HYLAND, T. (1979) 'Open plan — open education?,' *British Educational Research Journal*, 5, 2.

BERGER P. and KELLNER, H. (1981) *Sociology Reinterpreted*, Harmondsworth, Penguin.

BERLAK, A. *et. al.* (1975) 'Teaching and learning in English primary schools,' in HAMMERSLEY, M. and WOODS, P. (Eds) *The Process of Schooling*, London, Routledge and Kegan Paul/Open University Press, 1976.

BERLAK A. and BERLAK, H. (1981) *Dilemmas of Schooling: Teaching and Social Change*, London, Methuen.

BERNBAUM, G. (1979) 'Editorial introduction,' in BERNBAUM, G. (Ed) *Schooling in Decline*, London, Macmillan.

BERNSTEIN, B. (1975) 'Class and pedagogies: visible and invisible,' in BERNSTEIN, B. *Class, Codes and Control Vol. 3: Towards a Theory of Educational Transmission'*, London, Routledge and Kegan Paul.

BIGGS, E. (1965) *Mathematics in Primary Schools*, London, HMSO.

BLACKIE, J. (1967) *Inside the Primary School*, London, HMSO.

BLACKIE, J. (1974) *Changing the Primary School*, London, Macmillan.

BLENKIN, G. and KELLY, A. (1981) *The Primary Curriculum*, London, Harper and Row.

BLENKIN, G. and KELLY, A. (1983) *The Primary Curriculum in Action*, London, Harper and Row.

BLISHEN, E. (1973) 'Your children on their teachers,' *Where?*, 84.

BLYTH, W. (1965) *English Primary Education Vol. 1: Schools. Vol. 2: Background*, London, Routledge and Kegan Paul.

BOWLES, S. and GINTIS, H. (1976) *Schooling in Capitalist America*, London, Routledge and Kegan Paul.

BOYD, J. (1984) *Understanding the Primary Curriculum*, London, Hutchinson.

BOYDELL, D. (1978) *The Primary Teacher in Action*, London, Open Books.

BOYDELL, D. (1980) 'The organization of junior school classrooms: a follow-up survey,' *Educational Research*, 23, 1.

BOYSON, R. (1975) *The Crisis in Education*, London, Woburn Press.

CAIN M. and FINCH, J. (1981) 'Towards a rehabilitation of data,' in ABRAMS, P. *et. al.* (Eds) *Practice and Progress: British Sociology 1950–1980*, London, George Allen and Unwin.

CALVERT, B. (1975) *The Role of the Pupil*, London, Routledge and Kegan Paul.

Central Advisory Council for Education (1967) *Children and Their Primary Schools Vol. 1 and Vol. 2* (The Plowden Report), London, HMSO.

Centre for Contemporary Cultural Studies (1981) *Unpopular Education*, London, Hutchinson.

COOK, A. and MACK, H. (1971) *The Teachers' Role* (British Primary Schools Today), London, Macmillan.

Consultative Committee (1931) *The Primary School*, London, HMSO.

COOPER, I. (1981) 'The politics of education and architectural design: the instructive example of British primary education,' *British Educational Research Journal*, 7, 2.

COX, C. and BOYSON, R. (Eds) (1975) *Black Paper 1975: the Fight for Education*, London, Dent.

COX, C. and BOYSON, R. (Eds) (1977) *Black Paper 77*, London, Dent.

COX, C. and DYSON, A. (Eds) (1969a) *Fight for Education: A Black Paper*, London, Critical Quarterly.

COX, C. and DYSON, A. (Eds) (1969b) *Black Paper Two*, London, Critical Quarterly.

CROLL, P. (1981) 'Social class, pupil achievement and classroom interaction', in SIMON, B. and WILLCOCKS, J. (Eds) *Research and Practice in the Primary Classroom*, London, Routledge and Kegan Paul.

DALE, R. (1979) 'From endorsement to disintegration: progressive education from the golden age to the green paper', *British Journal of Education Studies*, 27, 3.

DALE, R. (1981) 'Control, accountability and William Tyndale', in DALE, R. et. al. (Eds) *Education and the State Vol. 2: Policy, Patriarchy and Practice*, Lewes, Falmer Press/Open University Press.

DANIELS, J. (1961) 'The effects of streaming in the primary school: I What teachers believe; II Comparison of streamed and unstreamed schools', *British Journal of Educational Psychology*, 31.

DAVIES, BRIAN (1976) *Social Control and Education*, London, Methuen.

DAVIES, BRONWYN (1982) *Life in the Classroom and Playground*, London, Routledge and Kegan Paul.

DEARDEN, R. (1968) *The Philosophy of Primary Education*, London, Routledge and Kegan Paul.

DEARDEN, R. (1976) *Problems in Primary Education*, London, Routledge and Kegan Paul.

DELAMONT, S. (1983) *Interaction in the Classroom*, London, Methuen.

DENSCOMBE, M. (1980) 'Pupils' strategies and the open classroom', in WOODS, P. (Ed) *Pupil Strategies: Explorations in the Sociology of the School*, London, Croom Helm.

Department of Education, Northern Ireland (1981) *Primary Education: Report of an Inspectorate Survey in Northern Ireland*, Belfast, DENI.

Department of Education and Science (1975) *A Language for Life* (The Bullock Report) London, HMSO.

Department of Education and Science (1978) *Primary Education in England — a Survey by HM Inspectors of Schools*, London, HMSO.

Department of Education and Science (1980) *A Framework for the School Curriculum*, London, HMSO.

Department of Education and Science (1981) *The School Curriculum*, London, HMSO.

Department of Education and Science (1982a) *Education 5 to 9: an Illustrative Survey of 80 First Schools in England*, London, HMSO.

Department of Education and Science (1982b) *The New Teacher in School*, London, HMSO.

Department of Education and Science (1983a) *Statistics of Education:*

Schools, London, HMSO.

Department of Education and Science (1983b) *Statistics of Education: Teachers in Service*, London, HMSO.

Department of Education and Science (1984a) *Statistics of Education: Schools*, London, HMSO.

Department of Education and Science (1984b) *English from 5 to 16*, London, HMSO.

DEWHURST, J. and TAMBURRINI, J. (1978) 'Team teaching in primary schools', *Education 3–13*, 6, 2.

DONALDSON, M. (1978) *Children's Minds*, Glasgow, Fontana.

DOUGLAS, J. (1964) *The Home and the School: A Study of Ability and Attainment in the Primary School*, London, MacGibbon and Kee.

EDE, J. and WILLIAMSON, J. (1980) *Talking, Listening and Learning*, London, Longmans.

EGGLESTON, J. (1977) *The Sociology of the School Curriculum*, London, Routledge and Kegan Paul.

ELLIS, T. et. al. (1976) *William Tyndale: The Teachers' Story*, London, Writers and Readers Publishing Cooperative.

EVETTS, J. (1973) *The Sociology of Educational Ideas*, London, Routledge and Kegan Paul.

FEATHERSTONE, J. (1971) *Schools Where Children Learn*, New York, Liveright.

FLOUD, J. and HALSEY, A. (1961) 'Introduction', in HALSEY, A., FLOUD, J. and ANDERSON, C. (Eds) *Education Economy and Society*, New York, Free Press.

FROOME, S. (1970) *Why Tommy isn't Learning*, London, Tom Stacey.

FROOME, S. (1975) 'Reading and the school handicap score,' in COX, C. and BOYSON, R. (Eds) *Black Paper 1975: The Fight for Education*, London, Dent.

GALTON, M. and SIMON, B. (Eds) (1981) *Progress and Performance in the Primary Classroom*, London, Routledge and Kegan Paul.

GALTON, M., SIMON, B. and CROLL, P. (1980) *Inside the Primary School*, London, Routledge and Kegan Paul.

GOFFMAN, E. (1968) *Asylums*, Harmondsworth, Penguin.

GOODACRE, E. (1968) *Teachers and their Pupils' Home Background*, Slough, NFER.

GRAY, J. and SATTERLEY, D. (1976) 'A chapter of errors: teaching styles and pupil progress in retrospect,' *Educational Research*, 19, 1.

GRETTON, J. and JACKSON, M. (1976) *William Tyndale — Collapse of a School or a System?* London, George Allen and Unwin.

HAMMERSLEY, M. (1977) *Teacher Perspectives*. Educational Studies: A Second Level Course: E 202 Schooling and Society Units 9 and 10, Milton Keynes, Open University Press.

HARGREAVES, D. (1967) *Social Relations in a Secondary School*, London, Routledge and Kegan Paul.

HARGREAVES, D. (1977) 'Power and the paracurriculum,' in RICHARDS, C. (Ed) *Power and the Curriculum: Issues in Curriculum Studies*, Driffield, Nafferton Books.

HEAD, D. (Ed) (1974) *Free Way to Learning*, Harmondsworth, Penguin.

HMSO (1983) *Teaching Quality* (White Paper); London, HMSO.

HOYLE, E. (1975) 'The creativity of the school in Britain', in HARRIS, A. *et. al.* (Eds) *Curriculum Innovation*, London, Croom Helm.

ILLICH, I. (1971) *Deschooling Society*, Harmondsworth, Penguin.

JACKSON, B. (1964) *Streaming: An Education System in Miniature*, London, Routledge and Kegan paul.

JACKSON, P. (1968) *Life in Classrooms*, New York, Holt, Rinehart and Winston.

JACKSON, P. (1971) 'The way teachers think,' in LESSER, G. (Ed) *Psychology and Educational Practice*, Glenview, Ill., Scott, Foresman.

JENCKS, C. *et. al.* (1972) *Inequality: A Re-assessment of the Effects of Family and Schooling in America*, New York, Basic Books.

JOHNSON, R. (1976) 'Notes on the schooling of the English working class, 1780–1850, in DALE, R. *et. al.* (Eds) *Schooling and Capitalism*, London, Routledge and Kegan Paul.

KANTER, R.M. (1972) 'The organization child: experience management in a nursery school,' *Sociology of Education*, 45, 2.

KELLY, A. (1981) 'Research and the primary curriculum,' *Journal of Curriculum Studies*, 13, 3.

KEMBALL-COOK, B. (1972) 'The garden of Plowden,' in BOYSON, R. (Ed) *Education: Threatened Standards*, Enfield, Churchill Press.

KING, R. (1978) *All Things Bright and Beautiful? A Sociological Study of Infants' Classrooms*, Chichester, Wiley.

KING, R. (1979) 'The search for the 'invisible' pedagogy,' *Sociology*, 13, 3.

KING R. (1983) 'On the diversity of primary education,' *Education 3–13*, 11, 2.

KOGAN, M. (1978) *The Politics of Educational Change*, Glasgow, Fontana.

LACEY, C. (1970) *Hightown Grammar*, Manchester, Manchester University Press.

LACEY, C. (1976) 'Problems of sociological fieldwork: a review of the methodology of "Hightown Grammar",' in SHIPMAN, M. (Ed) *The Organization and Impact of Social Research*, London, Routledge and Kegan Paul.

LEE, L. (1962) *Cider With Rosie*, Harmondsworth, Penguin.

LORTIE, D. (1975) *Schoolteacher: a Sociological Study*, Chicago, Chicago University Press.

MACLURE, J. (1968) *Educational Documents: England and Wales 1816–1968*, London, Methuen.

MAKINS, V. (1969a) 'Child's eye view of teacher,' *Times Educational Supplement*, 19 September.

MAKINS, V. (1969b) 'Child's eye view: the winners,' *Times Educational Supplement*, 26 September.

MARRIOTT, S. (1981) *Some Perspectives of Junior School Teachers*, unpublished thesis, University of Leicester.

MARSH, L. (1970) *Alongside the Child in the Primary School*, London, A. and C. Black.

McPHERSON, G. (1972) *Small Town Teacher*, Cambridge, Mass., Harvard University Press.

MEIGHAN, R. (1978) 'Consultation and educational ideologies: some issues

raised by research into children's judgment of teaching performance,' in
BARTON, L. and MEIGHAN, R. (Eds) *Sociological Interpretations of
Schooling and Education*, Driffield, Nafferton Books.

MEIGHAN, R. (1981) *A Sociology of Educating*, London, Holt, Rinehart and
Winston.

MEIGHAN R. and BROWN, C. (1980) 'Locations of learning and ideologies of
education: some issues raised by a study of "Education Otherwise",' in
BARTON, L., MEIGHAN, R. and WALKER, S. (Eds) *Schooling Ideology
and the Curriculum*, Lewes, Falmer Press.

MIDWINTER, E. (1974) 'Whose school?,' *Education 3–13*, 2, 2.

MILLS, R. (1980) *Classroom Observation of Primary School Children*,
London, George Allen and Unwin.

MORAN, P. (1971) 'The integrated day,' *Educational Research*, 14.

NASH, R. (1973) *Classrooms Observed*, London, Routledge and Kegan Paul.

NASH, R. (1980) *Schooling in Rural Societies*, London, Methuen.

NEWSON, J. and NEWSON, E. (1977) *Perspectives on School at Seven Years
Old*, London, George Allen and Unwin.

NIAS, J. (1984) 'The definition and maintenance of self in primary teaching,'
British Journal of Sociology of Education, 5, 3.

OPIE, I. and OPIE, P. (1959) *The Lore and Language of Schoolchildren*,
Oxford, Oxford University Press.

PARSONS, T. (1959) 'The school class as a social system: some of its functions
in American society,' in HALSEY, A., FLOUD, J. and ANDERSON, C.
(Eds) *Education, Economy and Society*, New York, Free Press, 1961.

PETERS, R. (1969) 'A recognizable philosophy of education': a constructive
critique,' in PETERS, R. (Ed) *Perspectives on Plowden*, London: Routledge and Kegan Paul.

PINN, D. (1969) 'What kind of primary school?' in COX, C. and DYSON, A.
(Eds) *Black Paper Two*, London, Critical Quarterly.

PLUCKROSE, H. (1979) *Children in Their Primary Schools*, Harmondsworth,
Penguin.

POLLARD, A. (1979) 'Negotiating deviance and "getting done" in primary
school classrooms,' in BARTON, L. and MEIGHAN, R. (Eds) *Schools
Pupils and Deviance*, Driffield, Nafferton Books.

POLLARD, A. (1980) 'Teacher interests and changing situations of survival
threat in primary school classrooms,' in WOODS, P. (Ed) *Teacher
Strategies: Explorations in the Sociology of the School*, London, Croom
Helm.

RAZZELL, A. (1968) *Juniors: A Postscript to Plowden*, Harmondsworth,
Penguin.

RAZZELL, A. (1979) 'Primary schools: a particularly raw deal,' in Rubinstein
D. (Ed) *Education and Equality*, Harmondsworth, Penguin.

REID, I. (1978) *Sociological Perspectives on School and Education*, London,
Open Books.

RICHARDS, C. (Ed) (1978) *Education 3–13*, Driffield, Nafferton Books.

RICHARDS, C. (1979) 'Primary education: belief, myth and practice,' in
BLOOMER, M. and SHAW, K. (Eds) *The Challenge of Educational
Change: Limitations and Possibilities*, Oxford, Pergamon.

RICHARDS, C. (Ed) (1980) *Primary Education: Issues for the Eighties*,

London, A. and C. Black.

RICHARDS, C. (1982a) 'Primary education 1974–80,' in RICHARDS, C. (Ed) *New Directions in Primary Education*, Lewes, Falmer Press.

RICHARDS, C. (Ed) (1982b) *New Directions in Primary Education*, Lewes, Falmer Press.

RIST, R. (1970) 'Student social class and teacher expectations: the self-fulfilling prophecy in ghetto education,' *Harvard Educational Review*, 40, 3.

ROBINSON, P. (1981) *Perspectives on the Sociology of Education: an Introduction*, London, Routledge and Kegan Paul.

ROBINSON, R. (1876) *Teacher's Manual of Method and Organization Adapted to the Primary Schools of Great Britain, Ireland and the Colonies*, London, Longmans Green.

ROGERS, V. (Ed) (1970) *Teaching in the British Primary School*, London, Macmillan.

RUBINSTEIN, D. (Ed) (1979) *Education and Equality*, Harmondsworth, Penguin.

School of Barbiana (1970) *Letter to a Teacher*, Harmondsworth, Penguin.

Schools Council (1983) *Primary Practice* (Working Paper 75). London, Methuen.

Scottish Education Department (1980) *Learning and Teaching in Primary 4 and Primary 7 — A Report by HM Inspectors of Schools in Scotland*, Edinburgh, HMSO.

SELLECK, R. (1972) *English Primary Education and the Progressives 1914–1939*, London, Routledge and Kegan Paul.

SHARP, R. and GREEN, A. (1975) *Education and Social Control: A Study of Progressive Primary Education*, London, Routledge and Kegan Paul.

SILBERMAN, C. (1970) *Crisis in the Classroom: the Remaking of American Education*, New York, Random House.

SILBERMAN, C. (Ed) (1973) *The Open Classroom Reader*, New York, Randon House.

SIMON, B. (1981) 'The primary school revolution: myth or reality?' in SIMON, B. and WILLCOCKS, J. (Eds) *Research and Practice in the Primary Classroom*, London, Routledge and Kegan Paul.

SKILBECK, M. (1976) 'Three educational ideologies,' in SKILBECK, M. and HARRIS, A. *Ideology, Knowledge and the Curriculum*, E203 Curriculum Design and Development Units 3 and 4, Milton Keynes, The Open University Press.

SLUCKIN, A. (1981) *Growing Up in the Playground*, London, Routledge and Kegan Paul.

START, K. and WELLS, B. (1972) *The Trend of Reading Standards*, Slough, NFER.

STEADMAN, S. *et. al.* (1978) *Impact and Take-up Project. A First Interim Report to the Programmes Committee of the Schools Council*, London, Schools Council.

STUBBS, M. (1983) *Language, Schools and Classrooms*, London, Methuen.

SUTHERLAND, A. (1981) *Curriculum Projects in Primary Schools*, Belfast, Northern Ireland Council for Educational Research.

TAYLOR, J. (1971) *Organizing and Integrating the Infant Day*, London,

George Allen and Unwin.

TREW, K. (1977) *Teacher Practices and Classroom Resources*, Belfast, Northern Ireland Council for Educational Research.

TYLER, W. (1977) *The Sociology of Educational Inequality*, London, Methuen.

WALKER, R. and ADELMAN, C. (1975) *A Guide to Classroom Observation*, London, Methuen.

WALKER, R. and ADELMAN, C. (1976) 'Strawberries,' in STUBBS, M. and DELAMONT, S. (Eds) *Explorations in Classroom Observation*, Chichester, Wiley.

WALLER, W. (1932) *The Sociology of Teaching*, New York, Wiley.

WHITBREAD, N. (1972) *The Evolution of the Nursery-Infant School*, London, Methuen.

WHITESIDE, T. (1978) *The Sociology of Educational Innovation*, London, Methuen.

WILLIAMSON, B. (1981) 'Contradictions of control: elementary education in a mining district 1870–1977,' in BARTON, L. and WALKER, S. (Eds) *Schools Teachers and Teaching*, Lewes, Falmer Press.

WILLES, M. (1981) 'Children becoming pupils: the study of discourse in nursery and reception classes,' in ADELMAN, C. (Ed) *Uttering, Muttering*, London, Grant McIntyre.

WILLES, M. (1983) *Children into Pupils*, London, Routledge and Kegan Paul.

WILSON, B. (1962) 'The teacher's role: a sociological analysis,' *British Journal of Sociology*, 13.

WILSON, P. (1973) 'Plowden children,' in DALE, R. *et. al.* (Eds) *Schooling and Capitalism*, London, Routledge and Kegan Paul, 1976.

WOODS, P. (1977a) *The Pupil's Experience*. Educational Studies: A Second Level Course: E 202 Schooling and Society Unit 11, Milton Keynes, Open University Press.

WOODS, P. (1977b) *The Ethnography of the School*. Educational Studies: A Second Level Course: E 202 Schooling and Society Units 7 and 8, Milton Keynes, Open University Press.

WOODS, P. (1979) *The Divided School*, London, Routledge and Kegan Paul.

WOODS, P. (1980) 'Strategies in teaching and learning,' in WOODS, P. (Ed) *Teacher Strategies: Explorations in the Sociology of the School*, London, Croom Helm.

WOODS, P. (1983) *Sociology and the School*, London, Routledge and Kegan Paul.

WRIGHT, N. (1977) *Progress in Education*, London, Croom Helm.

YOUNG, M. (1971) 'Introduction,' in YOUNG, M. (Ed) *Knowledge and Control*, London, Collier-Macmillan.

Author Index

Subject Index